1̃0̃0̃

FACTS

BRIGHTON

BRIGHTON

Steve Horton

Bedford, England

First published in Great Britain in 2021
by Wymer Publishing
www.wymerpublishing.co.uk
Wymer Publishing is a trading name of Wymer (UK) Ltd

First edition. Copyright © 2021 Steve Horton / Wymer Publishing.

ISBN 978-1-912782-78-9

Edited by Jerry Bloom.

The Author hereby asserts his rights to be identified
as the author of this work in accordance with sections
77 to 78 of the Copyright, Designs & Patents Act 1988.

All rights reserved. No part of this publication may be
reproduced or transmitted in any form or by any means,
electronic or mechanical, including photocopying, or any
information storage and retrieval system, without written
permission from the publisher.

This publication is sold subject to the condition that it shall not,
by way of trade or otherwise, be lent, re-sold, hired out or
otherwise circulated without the publishers prior consent in any
form of binding or cover other than that in which it is published
and without a similar condition including this condition
being imposed on the subsequent purchaser.

Typeset and Design by Andy Bishop / 1016 Sarpsborg
Printed by CMP, Poole, Dorset

A catalogue record for this book is available from the British Library.

Sketches © Becky Welton-Fodder & Amy McIsaac.

FACT 1
1901
BRIGHTON & HOVE UNITED

Brighton & Hove Albion were initially formed as Brighton & Hove United. However, before the new club had even played a match, the suffix was changed from United to Albion.

Following the collapse of the professional Brighton United club in 1900, their manager sought to generate interest for a semi-professional outfit. At a meeting in the Seven Stars pub on Ship Street in June 1901, the new club was formed. It was constituted of a committee whose members were known to be keen supporters of the game.

A number of local amateur players showed an interest in joining and negotiations soon began with players who had played professionally around the country. The club was accepted into the Second Division of the Southern League and a deal was agreed to play at the County Ground in Hove.

Due to objections from Hove FC, the United was dropped as a suffix and Albion added instead. The first game was a friendly against Shoreham at the Dyke Road enclosure on 7th September. The game was played there as the County Ground was unavailable and Albion won 2-0. The *Brighton Gazette* reported that the team, which was not at full strength, "gave a capital exhibition and made the most favourable impression."

FACT 2

1902
MOVE TO THE
GOLDSTONE GROUND

The club moved to the Goldstone Ground in 1902. They opted to look for a new home after repeated difficulties in securing the use of the County Ground for games.

Albion were first told the County Ground was booked in February 1902 and were invited by Hove FC to use the Goldstone. They had moved into the field overlooked by Goldstone House, owned by John Clark, the previous year. Clark paid for fences, gates and turnstiles, but insisted that his livestock could still graze on the pitch.

When this happened on four more occasions that season, a formal groundshare agreement was made for 1902-03. After two seasons, Hove moved to Hove Park, with Albion buying the lease for £40.

In its earliest days the Goldstone Ground was a genteel setting, as described by Simon Inglis in his book *Football Grounds of Great Britain*, published in 1996. A low wooden stand behind one goal was often frequented by women and children. Behind this there was a bicycle shed.

At the other end was a pond which the players kicked balls into so they were softened up. This was drained in the early 1920s so that the North Bank could be built. Although Albion thought about moving in the 1940s, the Goldstone remained their home until 1997.

FACT 3

1902
RECORD VICTORY

The club's all-time record victory was on 4th October 1902. They thrashed Brighton Amateurs 14-2 at the Goldstone Ground in the first qualifying round of the FA Cup.

It took Albion just five minutes to open the scoring, when Jock Caldwell converted a penalty. Hardman doubled the lead on the quarter hour and further goals from Barney Lee and Lohmann Harland gave Albion a comfortable 4-0 half time lead.

After the break Albion tore the amateurs apart, scoring a further nine times to lead 13-0. Ben Garfield scored a hat-trick and Lee got two more to complete his own treble. Frank Scott and West also got two goals each.

Stone scored two consolation goals for the opponents, but just before full time Caldwell scored his second penalty of the game to make the final score 14-2.

In the next qualifying round Albion hit double figures again, winning 12-0 at Shoreham. They then drew 5-5 at home to Grays before winning the replay 3-0. Their cup run eventually came to an end in the fourth qualifying round when they were beaten 1-0 at Ilford.

FACT 4
1903
PROMOTED AFTER
TEST MATCH VICTORY

Brighton were promoted to the First Division of the Southern League in 1902-03. After finishing second in the table, they beat Watford in a test match to secure their promotion.

There were only six sides in the second tier and they played each other twice. Albion won seven, drew one and lost two of their ten games and finished in second, level on points with Fulham but with an inferior goal average.

Promotion and relegation weren't automatic, with the top two sides having to face the bottom two from the first tier in test matches. This paired Albion with Watford, with the game scheduled for 27th April at the neutral venue of West Ham.

There was a crowd of just 300 but they witnessed a thrilling game. Albion were 3-0 up after only fifteen minutes, taking advantage of the opposition having both of their full backs unavailable due to injury. Watford managed to stem the Albion tide and got a goal back five minutes before half time.

Within ten minutes of the restart, Watford had drawn level. They even threatened to take the lead, but Albion managed to break away and score a fourth. As Watford pressed hard for another equaliser, Albion added a fifth. *The Sportsman* described them as having played "a capital game all around."

FACT 5

1904
BLUE AND WHITE STRIPES

Blue and white striped shirts were worn for the first time at the beginning of the 1904-05 season. This has been the predominant home colours ever since, although there have been times when the shirts have been blue or white.

Albion wore light blue shirts for their first two seasons then a darker shade. After escaping relegation in 1903-04, thirteen new players were signed in the close season and fans were treated to a new playing strip as well. The shirts brought some better fortune, with Albion finishing tenth out of eighteen teams.

Blue and white stripes remained Albion's colours for forty-four years then for three seasons, 1948 to 1951, they wore blue shirts with white sleeves. They then reverted to stripes until 1964, when the blue with white sleeves came back, this time for six years.

In 1970-71 and 1974-75 Albion wore white with blue trimmings, but for the rest of the decade were in blue and white stripes. Between 1980 and 1987 they played in blue shirts with white trimmings then went back to stripes.

In 2020-21 Albion wore a blue home shirt for the first time in 33 years. From 1987 to 2020 they had always played in stripes, although the thickness of the colours did vary.

FACT 6

1907
BERT LONGSTAFF

One of Albion's most respected players, Bert Longstaff, signed for the club in 1907. He would remain with Albion for fifteen years.

Prior to joining Albion as a 21-year-old, Longstaff played for Shoreham in the West Sussex Senior League. He started off with Albion as an inside forward but was soon used more frequently at outside right due to his pace and accuracy in crossing the ball.

Longstaff went on to play 443 games in all competitions for Albion. 356 of these were league games, although the club was only in the Football League for two seasons whilst he was there.

In total Longstaff scored 86 goals and was a member of the 1909-10 Southern League title winning squad. He scored in the 3-1 victory over Swindon that clinched the title and was also in the team that beat Aston Villa in the 1910 Charity Shield.

Longstaff was given a benefit game in 1913 and another in 1923, after he had left Albion and rejoined Shoreham. He played for them as an amateur until he was thirty-nine and was also a competent cricketer, appearing for Sussex's Second XI. He remained living in Brighton until his death in 1970 aged eighty-four.

FACT 7
1910 SOUTHERN LEAGUE CHAMPIONS

1909-10 was a tremendous season with the club winning the Southern League by a comfortable margin as well as the Southern Professional Cup.

After finishing third in 1907, Albion were seventeenth and then eighteenth in the next two seasons. Manager Jack Robson completely overhauled the side for 1909-10, recruiting a number of new players from the North and Midlands. There were thirteen new arrivals and only five retained from the previous season.

Albion made a promising start, avoiding defeat in their first six games. They retained a remarkable consistency throughout the season and had a settled side, with five players playing all 42 matches.

The title was clinched on 23rd April in the penultimate game. Needing just a point against nearest challengers Swindon, Albion made no mistake and took a first minute lead at the Goldstone Ground. They eventually won 3-1 in front of an enthusiastic crowd of 11,000.

Albion had clinched a title just nine years after the club was formed. They finished the season five points clear of Swindon and conceded just 28 goals all season. As well as the title they also won the Southern Professional Charity Cup, beating Watford 1-0 in the final at Stamford Bridge.

FACT 8
1910 CHARITY SHIELD WINNERS

As champions of the Southern League, Brighton & Hove Albion were invited to take part in the Charity Shield (now the Community Shield) in 1910. They shocked Aston Villa, beating the First Division champions 1-0 at Stamford Bridge.

Between 1908 and 1912, the traditional curtain raiser to the season took place between the champions of the Football League and Southern League. Albion were definitely the underdogs against Villa, who had just won their sixth league title.

A large contingent of Albion fans were present in the 8,000 crowd for the game, which took place on a Monday evening. In the first half Albion's players refused to be overawed by their opposition and were deservedly level at half time.

After the break, Albion continued to apply themselves well and were dominant in midfield. With fifteen minutes remaining Albion won a corner. Bert Longstaff's kick was cleared by the keeper but the ball fell to Bill Hastings, who passed to Charlie Webb to score.

The *Daily Mirror* reported that Albion had won a "splendidly contested game" due to putting "dash and wim" into their work. The players were met by an enthusiastic crowd when they arrived back in Brighton. Matchwinner Webb was an amateur at the time and would remain associated with the club until after the Second World War.

FACT 9
1914
LEST WE FORGET

During the 1st World War between 1914 to 1918, five Brighton & Hove Albion staff were killed serving their country. Four players lost their lives, as well as the club's groundsman.

The first casualty was groundsman Fred Bates, who volunteered as soon as hostilities started. He joined the Royal Scots Fusiliers and was killed in November 1914.

Albion continued playing in the Southern League in 1914-15 then suspended activities for the duration of the war. This led to many players signing up or later being conscripted in 1916.

Left half Jasper Batey was the first player to be killed, whilst serving as a messenger for the Army Cycling Corps in France in October 1915.

Charlie Dexter, Albion's left back, was killed in action at the Battle of the Somme the following year. Another killed at the Somme was Charlie Matthews, a reserve player who scored once in twelve appearances for Albion between 1912 and 1915.

The highest profile of Albion's players to lose their life was goalkeeper Bob Whiting. He signed from Chelsea in 1908 and made 320 appearances for Albion, including all 42 games in the 1909-10 title winning season. Whiting was killed in 1917 whilst attending to the wounded at Vimy Ridge.

FACT 10
1920
THE FOOTBALL LEAGUE THIRD DIVISION

Brighton were one of the founding members of the Third Division for 1920-21 when the Southern League merged with the Football League.

At a meeting of the Football League in Manchester at the end of May, it was agreed to absorb the Southern League as a newly formed Third Division. The only club from 1919-20 not included was Cardiff City, who were elected straight into the Second Division. The numbers were evened up to 22 by adding Grimsby Town, relegated from the previous seasons second tier.

Albion's first game in the new structure was a 2-0 defeat at Southend. It was the first of sixteen defeats on the road that season but form at the Goldstone Ground ensured they eventually finished in eighteenth place. This meant the club had avoided the need to apply for re-election and a potential return to the Southern League.

The Southern League had not disbanded, but instead split into two sections, one for England and one for Wales. Albion reserves entered and surprised everyone by winning it, finishing two points ahead of favourites Portsmouth reserves.

FACT 11

1921
SAME SCORER FOR
FIRST TWELVE GOALS

Albion were thankful to Jack Doran at the start of the 1921-22 season. The striker scored all over Albion's first twelve goals of the campaign.

Doran had been the leading scorer for Albion in the previous two seasons. He got ten in 1919-20 in the Southern League then 22 in the club's first Football League season.

Albion had a great start to the 1921-22 season, picking up seven points in their first four games. Doran got hat-tricks home and away against Exeter, as well as both goals in a 2-1 win at Southend. They then lost six games in succession. Doran scored the only two goals in this dismal run, against Swansea and Aberdare.

The losing streak ended with a 1-1 draw at home to Watford, in which Doran took his goal tally to eleven, but Albion then lost 1-0 at Charlton.

On 29th October, Doran opened the scoring in the return home fixture against Charlton before Andy Neil added a second to become the first other Albion player to score that season. It finished 2-0 and in the next game, Doran scored five as Albion thrashed Northampton 7-0 at the Goldstone Ground.

An injury sustained on Boxing Day limited Doran's appearances later in the season. However, he still finished as top scorer with 23 goals.

FACT 12
1923
CORINTHIANS: THE FIRST FA CUP OPPONENTS

The first round of the 1922-23 FA Cup, saw the club drawn against the famous amateurs of Corinthians, who were making their first appearance in the competition. The tie, which needed two replays, attracted huge interest around the country.

Corinthians' team was made of the best amateur players in the game, drawn from public schools and universities. After suffering heavily during the war, they entered the FA Cup to revitalise interest.

Highlights from the first-round tie at the Goldstone Ground on 13th January were shown in cinemas. Corinthians went ahead early in the second half, but Andy Neil's equaliser meant the teams had to meet again at Crystal Palace. That game also finished 1-1, with Albion taking the lead and extra time failing to separate the two sides.

The second replay took place at Chelsea's Stamford Bridge ground on 22nd January. In front of a crowd of 43,760 both sides had their chances in the first half, but after the break Albion began to take control. With fifteen minutes remaining Neil's shot hit the post but Cook scored the rebound to send Albion into the next round.

The three ties had attracted a total attendance of over 90,000, with the 23,642 crowd at the Goldstone a club record attendance at the time.

FACT 13
1929 RECORD SCORER LEAVES

Record goal scorer Tommy Cook left the club in 1929. He had been with Albion since 1921 and netted 123 goals in 209 appearances.

Cook made his debut at inside left during the 1922-23 season but was soon switched to centre forward. He was Albion's leading scorer in three of the next seven seasons and scored eight hat-tricks. He even earned an England cap in 1925, despite playing in the Third Division South.

As well as being a prolific footballer, Cook was a professional cricketer too. He scored 32 centuries for Sussex and when he left Albion in 1929, it was for the sake of his cricket career, taking up a role in South Africa.

After the Second World War, Cook became Albion's manager but struggled and they finished bottom of the league. Scarred by memories of a plane crash during the war that killed fellow crew members, he took his own life in 1950.

Cook was buried in the graveyard of the village church in Cuckfield. In 2020 Albion arranged for a memorial stone to be placed at his grave after the old one had fallen into disrepair.

FACT 14

1932
FORGETTING TO
ENTER THE FA CUP

An administration error meant the club didn't enter the FA Cup for the 1932-33 season in the normal way and they had to take their place in the qualifying rounds.

Albion's secretary Albert Underwood forgot to make the customary application for the club to be exempted from the competition until the first-round proper. It meant the only way they could compete was to enter at the first qualifying round stage.

The first tie at home to Sussex County League side Shoreham attracted 5,000 fans, more than had been to any league game so far. The amateurs were thrashed 12-0 and Albion went on to beat Worthing, of the same league, 7-1 at home in the next round.

In the third qualifying round Albion were drawn away to Hastings & St Leonards, who played in the stronger Southern Amateur League. In front of a record crowd of over 7,000 Albion cruised to a 9-0 victory.

Albion had to travel further for the final qualifying round when they were drawn against Barnet of the Athenian League. It was expected to be a tough game, but Albion won 4-0 at Underhill to make it to the competition proper, where even more drama awaited.

FACT 15
1933
JOINT RECORD NUMBER OF FA CUP TIES

After finding themselves in the FA Cup qualifiers due to the administration error in 1932-33, Albion weren't content at just making it to the first round. They enjoyed a giant killing run that took them to the brink of the quarter finals.

Albion were drawn away to Crystal Palace in the first round, winning 2-1 at Selhurst Park. They then came from two goals down to win 3-2 at Wrexham in a replay after the sides had drawn 0-0 draw at the Goldstone Ground.

In the third round Albion had a glamour home draw against Chelsea — semi-finalists the previous season. They stunned their First Division opponents, winning 2-1.

Albion faced higher division opposition at the Goldstone Ground again in the fourth round. The end result was more comfortable than the score line suggests, and they ran out 2-1 winners over Second Division Bradford Park Avenue.

West Ham were the opposition in the fifth round, with Albion getting another home draw. In front of a then record crowd of over 32,000 Albion took a two-goal lead in the first half, but the Hammers came back to draw 2-2. In the replay at Upton Park, Albion lost 1-0 to finally bring their amazing run of nine ties to an end.

FACT 16

1934
LEADING SCORER PLAYS
JUST TEN GAMES

The leading scorer in 1933-34 was Oliver 'Buster' Brown with fifteen goals. Amazingly these came in just ten appearances as Brown only joined the club in February.

When first choice centre forward Arthur Attwood developed appendicitis, Brown was signed from West Ham United. Despite looking overweight, he soon gained the appreciation of fans with his goalscoring exploits.

Brown's fifteen goal haul included two hat-tricks within the space of five days. The first of these was in a 6-0 win over Bournemouth & Boscombe Athletic at the Goldstone Ground on 21st April, Albion's biggest win of the season. The second on 26th April was in a 4-3 defeat at home to Exeter in the second replay of the Third Division South Cup semi-final.

Brown's fifteen goal haul was one more than Atwood's total had been when his season was ended through illness. Brown was Albion's leading scorer again the following season with 26 goals, but he left the club in 1937 and drifted out of the game altogether. He died in 1953 whilst still in his mid-forties.

FACT 17
1936
RECORD APPEARANCE HOLDER

In 1936 Ernie 'Tug' Wilson, who played more games for the club than anybody else, left the club. He had been there fourteen years and made 566 appearances in all competitions.

A former miner, Wilson was 23-years-old when he joined Albion in 1922 from Midland League side Denaby United. He soon established himself as the first choice outside left and remained there for thirteen seasons. He was awarded a benefit game in 1933 but continued to improve with age.

In 1935-36 Wilson lost his place to Bert Stephens and at the end of the season he left the club. 509 of his 566 appearances had been in the Third Division South, where he had also scored 67 goals. He was just short of his 37th birthday and retired from the professional game.

Although Wilson was originally from Yorkshire he remained in Sussex and opened a newspaper, confectionery, and tobacco shop. He also played local football for Vernon and was twelfth man and baggage carrier for Sussex County Cricket Club. He died in Hove in December 1955, aged 56.

FACT 18
1938 BRIGHTON POLICE CENTENARY

As part of the Brighton Police's centenary celebrations, a football match was played between teams of Sussex and German police officers at the Goldstone Ground.

The visit in August 1938 was part of an exchange programme that had seen police officers from Sussex travel to Germany earlier in the year. German officers then spent a week in Hove, accompanied by the Lord Mayor of Wuppertal, Dr. Friedrich. Their itinerary also included a visit to Lewes gaol and a greyhound meeting.

Tensions were rising between Britain and Germany at the time. There was plenty of opposition to the visit, with a planned day in Hastings being cancelled due to anti-fascist protests.

At a reception on the morning of the match the Mayor of Hove, Mr Hillman, said that he hoped sport could show further understanding and peace between the people of the two countries. Dr. Friedrich replied that paths of friendship should be used to settle differences.

The game was well attended and there were no protests. Prior to kick off, the German players gave a Nazi salute during their National Anthem. The Sussex officers won 3-2, avenging a heavy defeat suffered on their visit to Germany.

FACT 19
1940
18-0 DEFEAT

Although Brighton were beaten 18-0 by Norwich City in a wartime fixture, there were some extraordinary circumstances that led to the defeat, which isn't included in official club statistics.

The Football League was suspended due to the Second World War. Clubs could take part in regional competitions but all results are now classed as friendlies due to their ad hoc nature and the fact that guest players could be used.

For this game at Carrow Road that took place on Christmas Day, transport problems meant that just four Albion players made it to the ground. Of these, Joe Wilson was the only one with first team experience. They managed to add Jimmy Ithell, a Bolton player who was stationed locally. A member of Norwich's youth team was also used, with the remaining five players being volunteers from the crowd.

Albion trailed 10-0 at half time and conceded another eight in the second half. Four of the Norwich players got hat-tricks and Ithell scored an own goal.

Afterwards, manager Charlie Webb praised his players for never giving up. If there was one small consolation for Albion, it was that they didn't have to play again later on. Some fixtures that day were double headers, with sides meeting each other in both the morning and afternoon.

FACT 20
1942
BOMB DAMAGE

During the Second World War the Goldstone Ground suffered extensive damage when it was bombed during an air raid by the German Luftwaffe.

Between 1940 and 1944, Brighton & Hove were subjected to 56 air raids which left 198 dead, nearly 800 injured and 200 buildings destroyed. Three Albion home games were abandoned in the early stages of the war due to air raid warnings, with the crowd being able to disperse safely.

In August 1942 the Goldstone was hit during a raid, with the bomb exploding at the western end of the North Stand. It caused severe damage to the roof and girders and windows in the West Stand were blown out. The pitch was covered in debris but thankfully nobody was hurt. Albion were still able to fulfil their regional competition fixtures, often borrowing players from local army camps.

The roof of the stand had to be removed but it was replaced in time for the resumption of competition in 1946. Peacetime brought about huge crowds across the country and even though Albion struggled, they still attracted attendances of around 20,000 per game.

FACT 21
1946
CLUB CREST

Brighton first adopted a crest to wear on their shirts in 1946. It featured the coat of arms of both Brighton and Hove and is one of many the club have had over the years.

The shield of Brighton features martlets (a mythical bird), dolphins and coral. That of Hove contains martlets and a ship that has run aground, in commemoration of French raids on Sussex in the sixteenth century. This crest was used most seasons until 1975, although on occasions a simple shield with BHAFC was adopted.

In 1975, following the adoption of the nickname 'The Dolphins' a circle with a new crest featuring a dolphin in the middle was designed. However just two years later, after 'The Seagulls' took over as the nickname, the crest was changed again.

Following the takeover by Dick Knight in 1997, a shield shaped crest with a seagull inside was adopted the following year. This was because the new ownership sought to break from the past. As a one off in 2001-02, the Brighton & Hove shields were used as it was the centenary season.

When the club moved to the new stadium at Falmer in 2011, the crest was modernised again. It reverted back to a seagull inside a circle and has remained that way since.

FACT 22

1947
CHARLIE WEBB RETIRES

In 1947 one of the club's greatest ever servants, Charlie Webb, stepped down as manager. However, it didn't quite bring to an end his association going back forty years, as he stayed on in another position.

Webb initially looked set for a military career and was enlisted with the Essex Regiment, playing regimental football in Ireland. After a spell with Bohemians in the Irish League, he played for Albion as an amateur in 1909-10, making a key contribution in the Southern League success.

The following season Webb turned professional, and his goals tally was in double figures each season. However, an injury sustained in November 1914, coupled with the outbreak of war, ended his playing career.

Webb was a prisoner of war in Germany when he was offered the Albion manager's job. He took up his post on his demobilisation in 1919. His first season was in the Southern League then Albion became founder members of the Football League Third Division.

During 28 years as manager, Webb developed a reputation for finding players from the regional leagues. His sides played good football and challenged for promotion on occasions, but he also had fallouts with the board over their interference in team affairs. Webb stepped down as manager in 1947 aged sixty but remained as club secretary for a year before retiring.

FACT 23
1948
APPLYING FOR RE-ELECTION

After finishing bottom of the Third Division South in 1947-48, re-election to the Football League had to be applied for.

Tommy Cook replaced Charlie Webb as manager, but he was unable to replicate the magic of his playing days. Albion won their opening fixture 3-2 at Watford but then lost 5-0 at home to QPR, the first of three successive defeats.

After a 4-0 home defeat to Walsall in November, supporters demonstrated on the pitch. Cook was sacked and replaced by Don Welsh. However, he took time to turn things around and between September and January Albion went fifteen games without a win.

A run of seven games undefeated in the Spring lifted Albion out of the bottom two. With three games remaining they looked safe, but they lost them all and finished bottom, separated from two other sides only by goal difference.

Along with Norwich City who had finished in 21st position, they had to apply for re-election. There was no need to worry as at the vote on 20th May both clubs were comfortably re-elected, with none of the three non-league applicants receiving any votes.

FACT 24
1948 OLYMPIC HOST

When the Olympic Games were held in London in 1948, the Goldstone Ground was one of only two venues outside the host city to stage a match in the football tournament.

The two preliminary round games took place on 26th July at the Goldstone and Fratton Park in Portsmouth. They were essentially qualifiers for the main tournament, with the opening ceremony still three days away.

6,000 attended the game at Albion's ground between Luxembourg and Afghanistan. Jules Gales opened the scoring for Luxembourg after just six minutes, then Nicolas Kettel and Fernand Schammel scored in the closing stages of the first half to give them a commanding lead at the break.

Marcel Paulus scored a fourth for Luxembourg after an hour then Gales added another with eleven minutes to go. Paulus got his second and Luxembourg's sixth a minute later to complete the rout.

Five days later the tournament proper got under way and Luxembourg faced Yugoslavia at Fulham's Craven Cottage. Schammel gave Luxembourg a surprising lead after ten minutes and it remained that way at half time. In the second half the favourites hit back in devastating fashion, scoring six times without reply to progress to the next round.

FACT 25
1951
A CHRISTMAS DOUBLE OVER PALACE

Brighton played Crystal Palace on successive days over Christmas 1951. Albion proved triumphant in both matches, winning 2-1 at Selhurst Park and 4-3 at the Goldstone Ground.

The first game was at Selhurst Park on Christmas Day and Palace opened the scoring within a minute of kick off. In the last half hour Albion struck back. Jimmy Garbutt equalised from close range and then Billy Reed headed the winner in front of 15,323 spectators.

On Boxing Day a crowd of 24,228 were at the Goldstone Ground. This was three times as many as had watched the fixture the previous February and they witnessed a seven-goal thriller. Johnny McNichol scored Albion's winner in fading light, ten minutes from full time.

The back-to-back victories took Albion to the top of the Third Division South table. They had a two-point lead over Plymouth Argyle but had played a game more. However, Albion were unable to keep up the pace and eventually finished fifth.

FACT 26

1956
112 GOALS STILL
NOT ENOUGH

In 1955-56 112 goals were scored, more than any other league season in their history. However, it still wasn't enough for promotion, as they missed out by one point.

Albion failed to score in just six of their 46 games, all of those being away from home. At the Goldstone Ground they lost just once and averaged just over three goals per game. They scored five or more goals on five occasions and the biggest win was a 6-0 thrashing of Norwich City.

Despite Albion's goal scoring exploits, Leyton Orient led the way all season. Even though Albion won and drew against them in the spring, it remained the London team's title to lose. On 25th April, Albion lost 2-1 at third placed Ipswich. This confirmed Orient's promotion with a game still remaining.

The top three sides all scored over 100 goals. Albion finished with 112, Ipswich 108 and Orient 106. Albion's top scorer was Albert Mundy, who found the net 28 times. Frustratingly, Albion's total of 65 points was six more than Ipswich needed the following season to secure promotion.

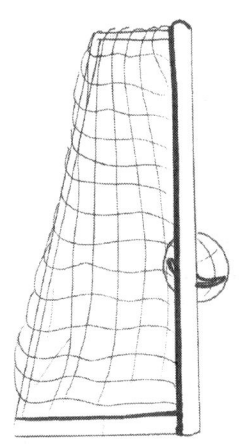

FACT 27

1958
THIRD DIVISION
SOUTH CHAMPIONS

In 1957-58 the club finally secured promotion to the Second Division. They went up after finishing as champions of the Third Division South.

With only one team going up every season from their division, Albion had been frustrated previously. They finished second in both 1954 and 1956, as manager Billy Lane built a side that gained a reputation for attacking, entertaining football.

At the start of 1957-58, Albion won six and drew one of their first seven games to go top of the table, only to lose four in a row. However, they recovered and were top at Christmas with a four-point lead.

During the Spring, Albion and Plymouth Argyle often exchanged places at the top. Albion though knew they'd have two games left to play once Plymouth had completed their fixtures. After the last day of the regular season Albion were second but knew a draw in one of their last two games would guarantee promotion.

The first of these was a 1-0 defeat at Brentford, who went top of the table themselves. This meant the pressure was really on when Watford came to the Goldstone Ground on 28th April. There were over 31,000 inside with many more locked out and Albion made no mistake. They won 6-0 to secure the championship and promotion for the first time in their history.

FACT 28
1958
OPENING DAY
RECORD DEFEAT

The club got off to the worst possible start to life in the Second Division. On the opening day of the season, they were beaten 9-0 at Middlesbrough, still a club record defeat today.

Albion could not have been given a harder start in their first ever game at this level. In front of a shirt sleeved crowd of 32,000 they went a goal down after conceding a penalty in only the fifth minute. By half time it was 4-0 and in the second half Boro' continued to show no mercy to the new boys, ending up 9-0 winners.

Striker Brian Clough, who would later manage Albion, got five of the goals in his determination to show he was still worthy of an England place despite not being in the top division.

Albion's defence had no answers to the home side's fast flowing attack and were saved by the woodwork on a couple of occasions. Under the headline BRIGHTON ROCKED, the *People* reported that Albion had been "shaken, rattled, rolled and rocked."

In their first home game, Albion drew 2-2 with Charlton but then lost 5-0 at Liverpool and 3-0 at Bristol City. They did improve though and eventually finished a creditable twelfth.

FACT 29
1958 RECORD ATTENDANCE

The club's record home attendance was set on 27th December 1958, when 36,747 packed into the Goldstone Ground for a game with Fulham.

This was the return game of a Christmas double header where opponents met each other on successive days. The previous day Albion had gone down 3-1 at Craven Cottage to a side that were eyeing promotion to the First Division.

It is fair to say that the game at the Goldstone Ground was not a classic, but the vast majority of the record crowd did go home happy. Albion's players were set up to frustrate the opposition, with Bertolini doing a brilliant man marking job on England international forward Johnny Haynes.

Midway through the first half Freddie Jones went on a mazy run before setting up Tommy Dixon to score the opening goal. He could have had a hat-trick before half time but was too slow to react when presented with chances.

Albion's second goal, early in the second half, was route one. As Fulham appealed for a penalty kick, the referee waved play on and the ball was pumped up field to Adrian Thorne, who beat the keeper with a fierce shot that went in off the post. Dixon made it 3-0 from close range with thirteen minutes remaining and it remained that way at full time.

FACT 30
1961
FLOODLIGHTS

Floodlights were installed at the Goldstone Ground in 1961. They were switched on for a friendly with Danish side Frem Copenhagen.

After Albion were promoted to the Second Division in 1958, it was clear ground improvements were needed to reflect their status. The West Stand was built first, then in the autumn of 1960 the board announced that work would soon begin to install floodlights and that, weather permitting, they should be ready by the beginning of the following year.

Albion's opponents for the first game under lights were Frem, a semi-professional side who played in the Second Division in Denmark. The game was on 10th April 1961 and the front of the match programme said, "Brighton & Hove Albion F.C. Ltd Present a Floodlit Match Albion versus Frem (Copenhagen)."

Frem impressed with their skill and ball control and took the lead after eight minutes with a stunning strike from thirty yards. In the second half, Frem's youngsters tired and inspired by South African inside left Denis Foreman, Albion mounted attack after attack. Bobby Laverick scored two and Jack Bertolini added another to give Albion a 3-1 victory.

FACT 31
1962
EASTER REVIVAL
CAN'T STOP RELEGATION

Brighton were relegated from the Second Division in 1961-62. A brief upturn in fortunes at Easter was too late to stop Albion dropping back to the third tier.

Albion failed to win any of their first five games, but form improved slightly and at the New Year they were in sixteenth place. However, a run of eight games without a win between January and March saw them drop to the bottom of the table.

With four games remaining Albion were four points from safety. The Easter weekend, in which teams traditionally played three games, was crucial in their bid to beat the drop. They responded well, beating Norwich and Plymouth in successive days at the Goldstone Ground.

Albion still had a mountain to climb, being two points behind Bristol Rovers and with an inferior goal average. On Easter Monday, a below par performance saw them lose 3-0 to Norwich at Carrow Road, meaning there was now no chance of escape.

League restructuring since Albion's promotion in 1958 meant that for 1962-63 they would be competing in a national Third Division, where things would get even worse.

FACT 32
1963
DOWN TO THE
FOURTH DIVISION

The slump continued in 1962-63 when they were relegated to the Football League's basement, the Fourth Division.

Albion had a promising start to the season, picking up five points from the first three games. However, a 2-0 defeat at Barnsley in the fourth game was the start of an eleven-match winless sequence.

Four months without a home win led to the dismissal of George Curtis in February. The board took their time looking for a successor and by the time Archie MacAulay was appointed, there looked little hope of survival.

MacAulay's first game in charge on 12th April was a 5-0 home defeat to leaders Northampton. This was the start of a three-match losing sequence over Easter in which Albion couldn't even score one goal. They were now third bottom but most worryingly the three teams above them had nine games remaining, while Albion had just five.

On 4th May an Albion side who were reduced to nine men by half time due to injuries, were beaten 4-1 at by Watford at the Goldstone Ground. It confirmed their relegation with two games remaining. It meant that for 1963-64 Albion would be playing in the Fourth Division, created by the merging of the regional north and south third tiers in 1958.

FACT 33

1965
FOURTH DIVISION
CHAMPIONS

The club's second season in the Fourth Division saw them promoted in 1964-65 as Champions. However, the title race went down to the wire and they still needed a point in their last game of the season just to guarantee promotion.

Albion were unbeaten all season at the Goldstone Ground and also scored 68 goals from their 23 games. Away from home they were not so prolific and lost on nine occasions.

In an extremely tight finish, only three points ended up separating the top five sides, four of whom could go up. As the season drew to a close, Albion knew there was no room for error, but did have the advantage of playing their last game after some others had finished their season.

On Monday 26th April, Albion faced Darlington at the Goldstone Ground. In front of a huge crowd of 31,423 Jimmy Collins opened the scoring in the nineteenth minute. Jack Smith headed a second and although Darlington pulled one back, Wally Gould made it 3-1 just after the break.

The victory meant Albion secured promotion and also went up as champions. However, they were also just three points clear of fifth place Tranmere who missed out.

FACT 34
1965
BARRY REES
KILLED IN CAR CRASH

The promotion season in 1964-65 was tinged with sadness when Barry Rees was killed in a car crash. The 21-year-old had only been with the club for two months when tragedy struck.

Rees joined Albion from Everton in January 1965, having made just four appearances in the First Division over two seasons. Albion paid £10,000 for the versatile player, who established himself in the side as a right half.

On Friday 26th March, Rees played for Albion in a 3-1 win over Southport at the Goldstone Ground. The following morning he set off early to drive to Rhyl, North Wales, where his parents lived. His Mini Cooper was involved in a head on collision with a truck in Nuneaton and he died on the way to hospital.

Rees had played twelve times for Albion, scoring once. Manager Archie Macauley described his death as a "terrible blow". He had been capped as a schoolboy by Wales and been a reserve for the Under-23's. Macaulay said that he believed Rees could have become a full Welsh international within one or two years.

1972
LATE PUSH SECURES PROMOTION

FACT 35

Being unbeaten in their last twelve games of 1971-72 meant that Brighton snatched the second promotion spot to go up alongside runaway Third Division leaders Aston Villa.

When Albion lost 2-1 at Bradford on 18th March, they were four points behind Bournemouth, who looked favourites to join Villa in the Second Division. The following week Albion beat Villa 2-1 at the Goldstone Ground, followed it up with a win over Torquay, then picked up a draw at Bournemouth in a game they couldn't afford to lose.

Albion then won 1-0 at Barnsley, beat Wrexham 3-2 at home and entered the top two after a 2-2 draw at Blackburn on 12th April. It was extremely tight though. Albion were six points behind Villa who looked certainties for promotion, but just a point ahead of both Notts County and Bournemouth with six games left.

There was little room for error but nine points out of a possible ten meant Albion needed just a draw at home to Rochdale in their final game. On 3rd May, a huge crowd of 34,766 saw John Templeman give Albion a fourth minute lead. The game finished 1-1, leading to a pitch invasion and players being kept from the dressing rooms for ten minutes by jubilant fans.

FACT 36
1973
RELEGATED BACK TO
THE THIRD DIVISION

The club's return to the Second Division was a disastrous one. In a season that included twelve straight defeats, they were relegated after finishing bottom of the table.

After opening with a 1-1 draw with Bristol City at the Goldstone Ground, Albion were then hammered 6-2 at Blackpool. Their first victory was in their fifth game and was one of only two between August and January.

A 3-0 defeat at Millwall on 11th November was the start of a run of twelve losses in succession, during which Albion managed just five goals. This left them rock bottom, eight points from safety with fourteen games to go. The dismal run was finally ended with a 2-0 win over Luton at the Goldstone on 10th February, but Albion then lost their next two games.

The Spring then saw a revival in which Albion went seven games unbeaten. This included victories over Orient, Huddersfield and Preston who were all hoping to avoid the drop themselves. This gave Albion a glimmer of hope, but they still trailed by three points with four games left.

Albion's fate was sealed with a 2-0 defeat at QPR in their penultimate game. Manager Pat Saward had overseen a valiant attempt at a miracle, but the damage of the twelve successive defects could not be overcome.

FACT 37
1973
BRIAN CLOUGH

Struggling Brighton stunned the football world in 1973 when Brian Clough was appointed as their new manager.

After just three wins in their opening twelve games of 1973-74, Albion were nineteenth in the table and only three points off the bottom. Pat Saward was sacked and at the beginning of November Clough was sensationally appointed as manager, with his trusted sidekick Peter Taylor as assistant.

Just two weeks earlier Clough had fallen out with the board and resigned his position at Derby County, where he had won the League Championship in 1972. It was a massive statement of intent by new Albion chairman Mike Bamber who pledged First Division football within five years.

Albion were unbeaten in Clough's first five games in charge. However, they then suffered a humiliating 4-0 home defeat to Walton & Hersham in the FA Cup. Bristol Rovers then thrashed Albion 8-2 at the Goldstone Ground. Albion eventually finished the season in nineteenth, exactly where they were when Saward left. Clough's continued media commitments and failure to move permanently to Sussex arguably played a part in this.

Clough's time at Albion came to an end in July 1974. Despite pleas from Bamber, the lure of a return to big time was too much and Clough became the new manager of newly crowned champions Leeds United.

FACT 38
1974
START OF THE PALACE RIVALRY

Brighton's rivalry with Crystal Palace began in the 1974-75 season. Albion won an opening day fixture 1-0 at the Goldstone Ground and the rivalry intensified as the decade went on.

Both clubs were founder members of the Third Division South in 1920, having been regular opponents in the Southern League. For the next four decades they played each other more seasons than not, but there was no real animosity between fans.

The first game of 1974-75 pitted the two sides against each other for the first time since 1963. Palace had just been relegated from the Second Division and were tipped to go straight back up under flamboyant new manager Malcolm Allison.

The home fans in Albion's biggest crowd for three years (26,235) gave manager Peter Taylor a standing ovation for remaining loyal to the club rather than follow Brian Clough to Leeds. Ian Mellor, a close season arrival from Aston Villa, scored a brilliant solo goal to give Albion victory in a game described by the *Evening Argus* as having "the cut and thrust carried through with the zest of deadly rivals."

During the rest of the decade the rivalry intensified as the two clubs were twice promoted together on their way to the First Division. In an added twist they were managed by former Tottenham teammates, Alan Mullery and Terry Venables. The rivalry remains just as intense today.

FACT 39
1976
PETER TAYLOR
RESIGNS

After two seasons in sole charge as manager, Peter Taylor left the club on 16th July 1976. He told reporters it was because he had failed to achieve his target of promotion within two years, but Albion were quick to announce his successor.

Taylor had refused to join Brian Clough when he took the Leeds United job in 1974. He was appointed as Albion manager but in his first season saw them finish a disappointing nineteenth. Things were much better in 1975-76 and they were fourth, missing promotion by just two points.

On 16th July Taylor surprisingly resigned from his post, telling the board he had set himself a target and not achieved it. Chairman Mike Bamber acted swiftly and within three hours had appointed Alan Mullery as the new manager. Taylor had nothing but good words for Bamber and said it was the toughest decision of his life. He left a good legacy, with two of his signings, Brian Horton and Peter Ward, going on to have successful careers with the club.

Taylor initially denied suggestions that he had resigned to join Clough in his new role at Nottingham Forest. However, the following month he did become Clough's assistant, with the partnership going on to have success at home and abroad.

FACT 40
1976
BRIAN HORTON
APPOINTED AS CAPTAIN

Prior to resigning as manager, Peter Taylor recruited midfielder Brian Horton. The twenty-seven-year-old would go on to have a huge impact at the club over the next five years.

Horton joined Albion from Port Vale for £30,000 in March 1976 and became skipper of the side straight away. When Alan Mullery came in as manager and said he needed to trim the squad, he made it clear Horton would not be one of those leaving.

Mullery had intended to continue playing but placed enough trust in Horton to be a leader on the pitch, allowing him to concentrate on management. Albion won promotion in 1976-77 and Horton was the club's player of the year, ahead of record-breaking scorer Peter Ward.

After a near miss in 1978, Albion were promoted to the First Division in 1979. Horton was named in the PFA team of the year and despite now being thirty years old, remained a key part of Mullery's plans for the topflight.

When Mike Bailey came in as manager in 1981, Horton's time at the club was up. In August that year he signed for Second division Luton, with Tony Grealish coming the other way. Horton would be back at Brighton for a brief spell as manager in the late 1990s.

FACT 41

1977
PROMOTED

Alan Mullery's first season in charge was a memorable one. There was some stunning football at the Goldstone Ground as they clinched promotion to the Second Division.

The appointment of thirty-four-year-old Mullery, who played for England in the 1970 World Cup, was a bold one. He had only retired from playing earlier that year but promised to give 100% and ensure that there would be no shirkers at the club.

Albion won nineteen and lost one of their twenty-three home games. They scored 63 goals and failed to find the net just once. There were huge wins against York (7-2) and Walsall (7-0) and they scored four goals on four other occasions.

Promotion was clinched with two games to spare, when Albion beat Sheffield Wednesday 2-1 at the Goldstone Ground on 3rd May. They eventually finished second in the table, three behind champions Mansfield and two ahead of also promoted Crystal Palace.

Chairman Mike Bamber promised that funds would be available to strengthen the squad. He said that unlike five years earlier, the club could afford to make new signings and did not need to rely on the players who got them up to keep them there.

FACT 42

1977
PETER WARD'S
RECORD SEASON

During the memorable 1976-77 season Peter Ward scored 36 goals. It was the highest total ever in a single season by a Brighton & Hove Albion player and the most by anybody in the Football League that campaign.

A former engine fitter for Rolls Royce, Ward signed from non-league Burton Albion. He made his debut in March 1976, scoring in the first minute of a 1-1 draw with Hereford United. He finished that season with six from nine matches and became an automatic starter in Alan Mullery's side.

From the first weeks of the season Ward was banging the goals in and attracting scouts from topflight clubs. He struck four in a 7-0 win over Walsall but Mullery refused to consider cashing in on him, describing him as "priceless." By the end of the season he was valued at fifty times the £4,000 that Albion had paid for him.

Two goals against Reading on 12th April took Ward's tally for the season to 33, breaking Hugh Vallance's record from 1929-30. His final total was 36 making him the top scorer across England's four divisions.

Ward remained at Albion until October 1980 when he joined Nottingham Forest. He failed to live up to expectations there and spent four months back on loan at Brighton in 1982 before settling in America.

FACT 43

1977
SEAGULLS

Although commonly referred to as the Seagulls, it was not until 1977 that this came about when fans chanted it at a game against Crystal Palace.

In the mid-1970s Albion had adopted the nickname of the Dolphins, which featured on the crest of the town of Brighton. The club crest changed in 1975 to reflect this, but events on 22nd October 1977 meant all that would change.

On that day Albion were at home to Crystal Palace. At the Bosun pub in West Street (now Molly Malone's) a group of Palace fans were said to have begun chanting their nickname of "Eagles." This led to Albion fans responding with chants of "Seagulls." Club director Derek Chapman was in the pub and that led to the move towards the nickname being changed again.

A seagull has now featured on Albion's club crest for over forty years, although in the centenary season of 2001-02 the traditional town crests were used on shirts. "Seagulls" is chanted by fans every game home and away and the club website can be reached via the domain www.seagulls.co.uk.

FACT 44

1978
MISSING OUT ON
GOAL DIFFERENCE

The Seagulls just missed out on a second successive promotion in 1977-78. Only two points separated the top four sides, with Albion agonisingly missing out on goal difference.

Albion were not daunted by playing at the higher level. They were unbeaten for their first eight games, winning six of them. Three successive defeats brought a reality check but they soon regained their form to keep in touch with the top three.

With six games remaining, Albion were four points adrift of third place. However, they closed the gap with seven points out of a possible eight, including a crucial 3-1 win over Tottenham.

By the last day of the season, Bolton were definitely up but the other two places were between Albion, Southampton and Tottenham, with the latter two facing each other. Albion needed to beat Blackpool at home and hope Tottenham lost at Southampton. In front of over 33,000 fans Albion held on for a 2-1 victory, but then heard it finished 0-0 at Southampton.

Despite the disappointment, there was huge acclaim given to Alan Mullery and the players. 56 points would have been enough for promotion in the previous two seasons, but this time it meant being denied on goal difference.

FACT 45
1979
PROMOTED TO
THE FIRST DIVISION

Promotion to the English topflight for the first time occurred in the 1978-79 season. They clinched promotion on a memorable last day of the season beating Newcastle United 3-1 at St James Park.

For this final game of the season at Newcastle on 5th May, Albion knew that a win would guarantee promotion, but a draw would probably be enough due to their superior goal difference. 10,000 Albion fans made the long journey north in the hope of seeing their team make history.

After fourteen minutes Brian Horton headed Albion into the lead from a corner. Peter Ward scored another from the edge of the area and two minutes before half time Gerry Ryan made it 3-0, slamming the ball into an empty net after Peter Sayer's shot had been blocked. Newcastle did pull a goal back with ten minutes remaining but that couldn't stop the Albion celebrations.

At the end of the game the players and coaching staff applauded their fans. As a chorus of *Sussex by the Sea* reverberated around the terraces a delighted manager Alan Mullery said, "It's a bloody marvellous feeling, we worked hard for this over the last three years. I'm looking forward now to the big time - Liverpool, Manchester United, Nottingham Forest, let them all come."

FACT 46
1979
A SHOCK FIRST TOPFLIGHT AWAY WIN

Brighton's first ever away win in England's topflight was achieved against the odds. They beat European champions Nottingham Forest 1-0 at the City Ground, ending their 52-game unbeaten home run.

Albion had struggled to adapt to life in the First Division and were bottom of the table, having lost six of their seven away games so far. They were given no chance of getting anything at Forest, whose last home defeat had been back in 1976-77 when they were in the Second Division.

Gerry Ryan gave Albion a shock lead in the twelfth minute, seizing upon an error by Larry Lloyd to score. On the stroke of half time Forest were awarded a penalty, but John Robertson's kick was saved by Graham Moseley.

In the second half it was one way traffic, but Brian Horton and Steve Foster were rock solid in defence. Mark Lawrenson, returning from injury, didn't put a foot wrong in midfield. Albion almost added a second late on with a rare attack, but Peter Ward's effort was just wide.

The win lifted Albion off the bottom and a delighted manager Alan Mullery said afterwards "My team gave me 150% today. Some were so shattered they could hardly walk in the dressing room." They went on to finish sixteenth, six points clear of the relegation places.

FACT 47
1980 SHIRT SPONSORSHIP ROW

The club became embroiled in a row over shirt sponsorship in October 1980 when they refused to change shirts so a game could be televised.

For the midweek game at Aston Villa, Midlands company ATV wanted to show brief highlights the following evening. Rules at the time stated that for televised games clubs must wear plain shirts without sponsors' logos.

Manager Alan Mullery discussed the situation with presenter Gary Newbon and decided that Albion had greater obligations to their sponsors than a regional television company. As such they took to the field wearing shirts adorned with the name of the airline British Caledonian. Albion were within their rights to do this, as teams were only obligated to wear shirts with no logo if they were to be the main featured game.

Newspaper reports stated that ATV had spent £1,000 setting up cameras at the game which were not used. Albion supporters would not have complained about the lack of highlights, as they crashed to a 4-1 defeat, with all of Villa's goals coming in a 21-minute spell.

FACT 48
1981
FOUR GAME WINNING RUN ENSURES SURVIVAL

In 1980-81 Brighton looked doomed to relegation. However, they took maximum points from their last four fixtures to secure their topflight status.

With four games remaining Albion were in the bottom three, two points from safety. A big advantage they had though was that all but one of their remaining fixtures were against teams who were also struggling.

On 18th April, Albion won 3-0 at already relegated Crystal Palace. They then beat Leicester 2-1 at the Goldstone Ground, leaving their opponents on the brink of the drop. Next up was a crucial trip to Roker Park to face Sunderland. Albion won 2-1 to lift themselves out of the bottom three meaning their fate was in their own hands on the final day.

It was a tense afternoon at the Goldstone Ground on 2nd May, when Albion needed to match Norwich's result to stay up. At half time against Leeds it was 0-0 but the 27,000 crowd, the biggest of the season, was relieved to hear Norwich were losing to Leicester. In the second half goals from Steve Foster and Andy Ritchie gave Albion a 2-0 win to complete their great escape.

1981
FACT 49 MARK LAWRENSON LEAVES FOR RECORD FEE

In the summer of 1981 Brighton received what was then their record transfer fee of £900,000 when Mark Lawrenson was sold to Liverpool.

Albion paid a club record £100,000 to sign Lawrenson from Preston North End in 1977. This was a considerable sum for a newly promoted Second Division club to pay for a defender only just out of his teens.

Although eyebrows were raised at the fee, manager Alan Mullery had no doubts, telling *Shoot* magazine "He is only 20, is big and strong and will make his mark in a big way."

During his first season, Lawrenson impressed with his calm composure and ability to bring the ball out of defence, raising the game of those around him. It was the same the following campaign, in which Albion were promoted, with his ability to read the game showing maturity beyond his years.

Early in 1979-80 Lawrenson suffered ankle ligament damage and was out for a few months. Gary Stevens established himself in defence but Lawrenson proved to be an excellent midfielder on returning to fitness.

Lawrenson did not seek a move from Albion, but in the summer of 1981 the club needed to raise funds. European champions Liverpool paid £900,000 for him and he formed a solid defensive partnership there with Alan Hansen.

FACT 50
1982 HIGHEST LEAGUE FINISH

The highest league finish came in 1981-82. They overcame the sale of Mark Lawrenson and resignation of Alan Mullery to finish thirteenth in the First Division.

During the summer of 1981 Alan Mullery sensationally resigned as manager, angered by the sale of Mark Lawrenson to Liverpool and boardroom suggestions over the role of coaching staff.

Mullery's replacement was former Charlton boss Mike Bailey, who immediately set out to tighten Albion's defence. This meant that the football on offer was less entertaining than in previous seasons and despite results improving, crowds dropped.

Memorable results during the first half of the season included a first ever league victory over Tottenham and 3-3 draw at the Goldstone Ground with Liverpool, with Albion coming back from 3-1 down. In early March, a 1-0 win at Liverpool lifted Albion to eighth and had them dreaming of European football the following season.

Albion failed to build on the win at Liverpool. Bailey adopted a more attacking style but it was coupled with a downturn in results. They won only two of the last fourteen games to finish thirteenth. It remains Albion's best ever league finish, but the following season would end up being the most memorable one ever.

FACT 51
1983
RELEGATED

After four years in the First Division the club was relegated in 1982-83. A managerial change couldn't bring about an upturn in results as their away form cost them dearly.

Albion's squad looked good enough to survive. However, there was uncertainty around the club with reports that two key players, Steve Foster and Michael Robinson, had submitted transfer requests. Falling gates also meant that there was no money to boost the squad.

At the Goldstone Ground, Albion remained unbeaten until November, but their away form was abysmal. The first three away games were all lost with fourteen goals conceded and none scored. Mike Bailey was sacked in the first week of December after four successive defeats and he was replaced by chief scout Jimmy Melia, initially on an interim basis.

Melia's first game in charge was a 3-0 home win over Norwich, but Albion didn't win any of their next ten. A 2-1 victory at fellow strugglers Swansea on 1st March sparked a mini revival. This, coupled with FA Cup progress, led to Melia's appointment being confirmed in the middle of March.

Despite Melia's claiming Albion were too good to go down, they won only two of their last twelve fixtures. Relegation was confirmed with a 1-0 home defeat to Manchester City in their penultimate game on 7th May.

FACT 52
1983
AN UNFORGETTABLE
RUN TO WEMBLEY

Despite relegation in 1982-83, supporters enjoyed some unforgettable moments in the FA Cup, in which they defied the odds to reach the final.

The run was almost over before it started, when Albion were held 1-1 at home by Newcastle in the 3rd round. They won the replay 1-0 and then beat Manchester City 4-0 at home in the 4th round.

Albion were then drawn away to league leaders Liverpool. Few gave them a prayer but Gerry Ryan opened the scoring after half an hour. With twenty minutes left Liverpool equalised but Jimmy Case scored with a stunning strike almost immediately. Albion survived an onslaught that included a missed penalty, but they held on to reach the quarter finals for the first time.

Case was the hero again, scoring the only goal of the game in a 1-0 win over Norwich in front of a sell-out crowd at the Goldstone Ground. The semi-final draw then paired Albion with Second Division Sheffield Wednesday.

On 16th April at Arsenal's Highbury Stadium, Albion were ahead at halftime thanks to a goal by Case. Wednesday hit back but with twelve minutes remaining Michael Robinson scored the goal that took Albion to Wembley. First Division survival looked unlikely but that didn't stop the celebrations amongst jubilant players and supporters.

FACT 53

1983 AND SMITH MUST SCORE

Albion came so close to glory in the 1983 FA Cup final. The score was 2-2 with just seconds of extra time remaining as Gordon Smith had a clear run at goal, but his shot was saved by Manchester United keeper Gary Bailey.

Albion led 1-0 at half time thanks to a fourteenth minute headed goal from Smith. However, Frank Stapleton and Ray Wilkins scored in the second half as United looked destined to win the trophy. With three minutes remaining, Gary Stevens equalised from close range following a corner to take the game into extra time.

There was just a minute to go when Smith, superbly positioned just outside the six-yard box, received the ball from Michael Robinson. Radio 2 commentator Peter Jones excitedly shouted "And Smith must score" but his shot was smothered by Bailey.

Seconds later the referee blew the whistle for full time, meaning the two sides would be back at Wembley five days later for a replay. Jones's famous quote has remained in Albion folklore and became the title for one of the club's fanzines.

FACT 54

1983
CAPTAIN BACK BUT
ALBION LOSE REPLAY

Steve Foster returned to captain the side for the 1983 FA Cup final replay after being suspended for the first game. However, there was no fairy tale end to the season as Albion were beaten 4-0 by Manchester United.

A booking during a 1-0 defeat at Notts County on 30th April meant Foster picked up a two-game ban after totting up too many disciplinary points. The ban did not come into effect straight away meaning he was suspended for the last league game of the season and the final.

Albion appealed to the Football Association for some discretion but they refused to budge in any way. An application was made to the High Court but after a five-hour hearing Foster's ban was upheld.

Tony Grealish stood in as captain for the first game, where Foster was welcomed into the dressing room to offer encouragement to his teammates. Grealish led the team out wearing a headband, in tribute to Foster's trademark headwear.

Sadly for Foster and Albion the replay was nowhere near as good a contest as five days earlier. United were three goals ahead at half time and eventually ran out 4-0 winners.

FACT 55
1984
KNOCKING LIVERPOOL OUT AGAIN

In the fourth round of the FA Cup in 1983-84, Brighton showed that lightning can strike twice. They beat league leaders Liverpool 2-0 at the Goldstone Ground thanks to two goals in two minutes during the second half.

Albion rode their luck at times in the first period. Michael Robinson, who they had sold to Liverpool the previous summer, had an effort cleared off the line by Steve Foster. Joe Corrigan also made some key saves to keep the Reds at bay, saving from Ian Rush in a one on one and diving at full stretch to deny Steve Nicol.

In the 57th minute the Goldstone erupted when Tony Grealish played a perfect chipped pass to Gerry Ryan, who kept his cool to slot the ball past Bruce Grobbelaar. Just a minute later Steve Penney's through ball found Terry Connor who lifted the ball over the advancing Grobbelaar into the net.

It was by far the highlight of the season for Albion, who were beaten at Watford in the following round. During the campaign Jimmy Melia resigned as manager and was replaced by Chris Cattlin, under whom they finished ninth in the Second Division. There were also changes in the boardroom at the end of the season, with Mike Bamber stepping down as chairman.

1984
STEVE FOSTER LEAVES

FACT 56

Steve Foster, captain during the unforgettable 1982-83 season, left the club in 1984.

Foster signed from Portsmouth in 1979 and soon established himself as a favourite with the crowd in Albion's first season in the topflight. Such was his worth to the club that he was given a ten-year contract in 1981.

With his beard and headband that was worn to prevent an old wound from reopening, Foster was one of the most easily identifiable figures in football at the time. In 1982 Foster was capped by England and played one game in that year's World Cup.

In 1982-83 Foster captained the club to the FA Cup final against Manchester United but famously missed the Wembley occasion as he was suspended. He was available for the replay that Albion lost 4-0. Despite relegation, Foster remained at Albion for the upcoming campaign in the Second Division.

After Jimmy Melia resigned in October 1983, there was a much-publicised rift between Foster and new manager Chris Caitlin. However, when Aston Villa bid £200,000 for him in March, he insisted it was the lure of the First Division that tempted him away. He told the *Daily Mirror* that he would have stayed at the Goldstone Ground if Albion had a chance for promotion.

FACT 57
1985
END OF THE
'LEGO STAND'

There was a slight reduction in capacity at the Goldstone Ground in 1985. The West Stand extension, commonly referred to as the 'Lego Stand' was taken down after six years in use.

Following promotion in 1979, an extension to the West Stand, which was only two thirds the length of the pitch, was built to provide extra capacity. Seating 980, the box shaped structure earned the nickname of the 'Lego Stand' from many.

Writing in *The Football Grounds of England and Wales*, Simon Inglis described it as an "awkward neighbour" that was "tall, with six scaffolding pillars at the front."

By 1985 Albion were back in the Second Division and crowds were falling across the country. Even when there was an outside chance of Albion achieving promotion on the last day of the 1984-85 season, only 13,184 turned up at the Goldstone Ground.

During the summer the structure was dismantled and sold to Worthing FC, whose main stand had burnt down earlier in the year. At the time they were managed by Barry Lloyd, who would take charge at Albion less than two years later.

FACT 58
1987
BACK TO THE
THIRD DIVISION

The Seagulls had a terrible second half of the season in 1986-87, leading to them finishing bottom of the table. It meant they were back in the Third Division ten years after leaving it.

Alan Mullery was appointed as manager in the summer, but he was unable to rekindle the form of his first spell in charge. He was sacked in January with the club struggling in the lower half of the table and replaced by his assistant Barry Lloyd.

A run of twelve games without a win left Albion adrift at the bottom, ten points from safety with six games remaining. A 2-0 win over Crystal Palace at the Goldstone Ground on Easter Monday gave Albion a lifeline, but a 1-1 draw at Blackburn left them a mountain to climb. They then lost 1-0 at fellow strugglers Hull City, leaving them on the brink.

Just 5,377 turned out to see Albion's 2-0 home win over Sheffield United on 2nd May. This meant staying up was mathematically possible but only a freak set of results would allow it. Two days later, Albion's fate was sealed with a 2-0 defeat at Bradford City.

Despite being unable to save them from the drop, the board kept their faith in Lloyd and it proved to be the right decision.

FACT 59

1988
STRAIGHT
BACK UP

In 1987-88 the board's decision to keep faith in Barry Lloyd paid off. They won promotion back to the Second Division at the first attempt.

Albion was Lloyd's first managerial appointment in the Football League and he wasn't afraid to introduce his own idea and bring new players in. Among those let go was defender Darren Hughes, who Alan Mullery had paid £30,000 for the previous season.

Six new players were signed, including strikers Kevin Bremner and Garry Nelson. Goals had been hard to come by during the relegation season but the new strike pairing was prolific. Nelson finished the season with 32 goals, the first Albion player to get more than twenty in a season since Michael Robinson in 1980-81.

Promotion was secured on 7th May with a 2-1 victory over Bristol Rovers. Bremner and Nelson got the goals in front of 19,800 fans at the Goldstone Ground, the biggest league crowd there for five years. It meant Albion finished in second place and went up along with Sunderland and Walsall.

FACT 60

1988 GOALKEEPER TROUBLE

When Brighton faced Bournemouth at the Goldstone Ground on 10th September 1988, they almost took the field without a goalkeeper. Thankfully John Keeley was located just fifteen minutes before kick-off.

The day before the game, first choice keeper Keeley injured a finger. Communication errors led to reserve keeper Perry Digweed not being told that he was playing and the drama unfolded.

Alarm bells rang when the kick-off neared without Digweed — who lived in London — having even contacted the club to say he was having travel delays. Club officials desperately tried to get hold of Keeley, tracking him down to a pub where he had drunk four pints of beer.

Keeley was rushed to the ground where he took his place between the sticks. Albion lost the game 1-0, their third straight loss since the start of the season.

Digweed was at the Goldstone Ground on 21st September for a game with West Bromwich Albion. After half an hour he suffered a serious groin injury in a collision with an opposition player, which led to him being ruled out for the rest of the season. Albion had to make do with a number of loan signings until Keeley was available again in the New Year.

FACT 61

1989
FIVE PENALTIES
IN A GAME

When Albion played Crystal Palace at Selhurst Park on Easter Monday 1989, the referee awarded a Football League record of five penalties. Amazingly they were all within a period of just 27 minutes and of the four awarded to Palace, three were missed.

Albion were the underdogs in this game against a Palace side chasing promotion. Ian Wright put the home side ahead midway through the first half and in the 38th minute Mark Bright scored from the spot after he was fouled in the area.

Albion conceded another penalty soon after when Eddie McGoldrick was fouled by Dean Wilkins. However, keeper John Keeley guessed correctly and dived to his left to push Bright's kick away for a corner. From that set piece, Bright was fouled and the referee awarded another penalty. This time Wright was the taker but his kick came back off the post.

Ten minutes into the second half Kevin Bremner was fouled in the box and Alan Curbishley stepped forward to score the resultant penalty kick, making it 2-1. In the seventieth minute Ian Chapman handled in the area and John Pemberton became Palace's third penalty taker of the afternoon. His kick sailed way over the bar.

Albion almost snatched an unlikely equaliser near the end but Curbishley's shot from inside the six yard box was tipped over the bar.

FACT 62
1991 PLAYOFF FINALISTS

Brighton missed out on promotion back to the First Division in 1990-91 when they were beaten in the playoff final at Wembley.

Expansion of the topflight to 22 clubs meant four promotion places were up for grabs that season. However, Albion rarely looked likely to push for one of the three automatic spots. They lost eighteen of their forty-six games and finished with a goal difference of minus six.

Qualification for the playoffs was only confirmed in the last minute of the season, when Dean Wilkins' goal from a free kick gave them a 2-1 win over Ipswich at the Goldstone Ground. This set up a two-legged semi-final against Millwall, with Albion at home in the first leg.

On 19th May, Albion fell behind after fourteen minutes but stormed back to win 4-1. Three days later at The Den, Albion trailed 1-0 at half time but again came from behind to claim a 2-1 victory.

Albion's opponents for the final were Notts County, who had finished ten points ahead of them in the league. County took the lead after half an hour then Albion were twice denied by the woodwork. In the second half though Albion were overwhelmed, and County ran out 3-1 winners to claim a second successive promotion.

FACT 63
1992
RELEGATED TO
THE SAME DIVISION

A year after missing out on promotion to the topflight, Brighton were relegated back to the third tier. However due to the creation of the Premier League, the old Third Division was renamed the Second Division.

Already frustrated by player sales needed to balance the books, Albion's fans were further demoralised by five defeats from six games in October. They voted with their feet and just 4,420 turned out for a home game with Grimsby on 6th November.

A 4-1 defeat at Bristol Rovers on 20th April left Albion on the brink with three games to go. Four points from their next two games, both at home gave them a fighting chance. However, the last match was away to Champions Ipswich and even if Albion won, they needed others to drop points.

Before the game Ipswich were presented with the trophy and they were in no mood to ease up, taking a two-goal lead. Albion did pull one back before half time but their fate was sealed with seven minutes remaining when Ipswich scored a third.

Even though they had been relegated, Albion found themselves playing in the Second Division in 1992-93. This was due to the renaming of the Second to Fourth Divisions following the formation of the Premier League.

FACT 64
1995 INTERTOTO CUP HOSTS

The closest Brighton & Hove Albion fans have ever come to witnessing European club football was in 1995. That year the Goldstone Ground hosted Intertoto Cup games for Tottenham and Wimbledon.

The FA had misjudged the mood of clubs when they took three places for that summer's competition, which provided a long-winded route to the UEFA Cup. Only Wimbledon showed any interest and eventually, under threat of wider action against English clubs, Sheffield Wednesday and Tottenham reluctantly agreed to take part.

All three English participants played their games at lower league grounds, with Albion agreeing to let the Goldstone be used for home games for the two London clubs. The first game was on 24th June, when 1,879 watched Wimbledon beaten 4-0 by Turkish side Bursaspor. The following day 2,497 turned out to see Tottenham lose 2-0 against Lucerne of Switzerland.

By the time Wimbledon played their next 'home' game on 15th July they had little chance of progressing beyond the group stage. In front of just 702 fans a side containing only three players with first team experience drew 0-0 with Beitar Jerusalem.

The last Intertoto Cup game to be played there was on 16th July, when 2,143 saw Spurs lose 2-1 to Swedes Osters IF to confirm their elimination from the competition.

FACT 65
1995
ENGLISH FOOTBALL'S
OLDEST OUTFIELD PLAYER

At the start of the 1995-96 season Brighton had the oldest outfield player in English professional football on their books. Jimmy Case was 41 years and 6 months old when he gave up playing so he could concentrate on managing the club.

Case, a legend of the run to the FA Cup final in 1983, remained at the club despite their relegation. He joined Southampton in March 1985 and continued playing topflight until 1991, when he was 37 years old.

After spells with Bournemouth, Halifax and Wrexham, Case joined Albion as a player-coach in December 1993. At the start of the 1995-96 season, Case was the oldest outfield player registered at any club in the Premier League and Football League. Coventry City goalkeeper Peter Shilton was 46, but he failed to make any appearances, so Case remained the oldest active player.

Case's playing career ended abruptly when he suffered a neck injury in a reserve game with Arsenal that led to him being admitted to hospital. He decided to call it a day in early November, having made 159 of his 632 Football League appearances for Albion. By the end of the month manager Liam Brady had been sacked and he was appointed as manager.

FACT 66
1996
RELEGATED TO THE BOTTOM TIER

Brighton were relegated to English football's fourth tier in 1996. They finished second from bottom of the table and faced an uncertain future.

Albion won just three of the first fifteen matches and were in the relegation zone at the beginning of November 1995. Liam Brady departed as manager, following disagreements over how the club was being run. He was replaced by Jimmy Case but he was unable to turn the playing fortunes around.

Off the pitch, the shareholders and chief executive David Bellotti were making it clear that the only way the club could survive was if the Goldstone Ground was sold. With a groundshare at Portsmouth looking likely, there were regular supporter protests.

Relegation was confirmed with a 2-1 defeat at Notts County when there were still two games remaining. Albion's final home game, at home to York, was abandoned in the first half following a pitch invasion. It was replayed at 11am on a Thursday morning, with York winning 3-1 to avoid relegation themselves.

During the summer a consortium led by Brady tried to buy the club but the owners refused to sell. Albion would start 1996-97 in the bottom tier for the first time since the 1960s and with the prospect of soon becoming homeless.

FACT 67
1997 SALE OF THE GOLDSTONE GROUND

With Brighton's very existence in jeopardy, the inevitable sale of the Goldstone Ground went ahead in 1997.

Despite the protests in the 1995-96 season, the sale of the ground was still agreed by chairman Bill Archer and chief executive David Bellotti without any supporter consultation. The club was in danger of bankruptcy, but Archer stood to personally gain financially from the deal.

Supporter protests continued and Albion were deducted two points after a pitch invasion in October 1996. Fans of other clubs rallied around and in February 1997 a game against Hartlepool was dubbed 'Fans United' as supporters of clubs from around the country attended in solidarity. Albion's players responded and produced their best performance of the season, winning 5-0.

The last game at the Goldstone Ground was on 26th April. Incoming chairman Dick Knight was present and given an ovation by supporters, but his agreed takeover had come too late to prevent the sale.

In front of 11,341 fans, Albion beat Doncaster 1-0 to lift themselves off the bottom of the table and ensure Football League survival was in their own hands. Afterwards there was a pitch invasion with fans digging up sods of turf as souvenirs. The Goldstone Retail Park now stands on the site.

FACT 68

1997
HEREFORD OR BUST

On 3rd May 1997 Brighton drew 1-1 at Hereford United. The result meant they avoided relegation from the Football League and most likely saved the club from extinction.

Running alongside the off-field problems, Albion had a terrible run of form in the first half of 1996-97. They won just three of their first 22 games, leading to the dismissal of manager Jimmy Case. He was replaced in December by Steve Gritt, who took over a side eleven points adrift at the bottom of the table.

Slowly Albion closed the gap. Form at the Goldstone Ground, where they didn't lose any games under Gritt, was key to the revival. A 1-0 win over Doncaster in the last game at the ground on 26th April lifted them off the bottom.

Albion's final match was a do or die encounter at Hereford, where a win or draw would guarantee safety. Defeat would save Hereford and condemn Albion to non-league football with nowhere to call home.

A twentieth minute own goal by Kerry Mayo meant Albion trailed at half time. However, after an hour Craig Maskell's effort hit the post and Robbie Reinelt scored the rebound. The last half an hour seemed an eternity as Hereford pressed forward but Albion held on for the point they so desperately needed.

FACT 69
1997 HOME GAMES AT GILLINGHAM

With the Goldstone Ground now sold, Brighton began the 1997-98 season playing home games seventy miles away in Gillingham.

When it was confirmed that Albion would be leaving the Goldstone Ground, Portsmouth looked the likely venue for home games. This was soon ruled out due to fan opposition but the eventual option involved either a ninety minute drive or two hour trek by train.

The first home game at Priestfield was against Macclesfield on 16th August. Just 2,336 fans watched a 1-1 draw and afterwards manager Steve Gritt said "Did it feel like we were playing at home today? Well the seats were blue, like the Goldstone, but that's all".

Unbelievably, chief executive David Bellotti attended the game, despite pleas for him to stay away. Within weeks he was gone as Dick Knight completed his takeover of the club. However, a plan to groundshare with Millwall, far more accessible by train, was rejected by the Football League.

Albion continued to play home games at Gillingham for two seasons. They won just eleven of their 46 league fixtures there and attendances rarely reached the 3,000 mark.

FACT 70
1998
23RD AGAIN

The Seagulls again finished second from bottom of the Football League in 1997-98. This time though they were never in danger of relegation due to the terrible form of bottom club Doncaster.

Albion failed to win any of their first eight games, with Priestfield not being the same fortress that the Goldstone Ground had been in the second half of 1996-97. After beating Rochdale at 'home' in their ninth game, Albion then won 3-1 at winless Doncaster. This result left them 21st in the table, six points off the bottom.

Despite then going nine games without a win and scoring only three goals, Albion retained that six-point cushion. They then lost just one out of six, meaning that by New Year they were second bottom but twelve points ahead of Doncaster.

Albion won only two more games all season, finishing on 35 points. This was twelve less than the previous season when they almost dropped out of the Football League. This time they had been saved by woeful Doncaster, who won only four games all season, amassing just twenty points.

FACT 71
1999 RETURN FROM EXILE

Brighton returned to their hometown for the 1999-00 season, agreeing a deal to play at an athletics stadium in the suburb of Withdean.

There was no disputing that the stadium was far from ideal for football, but Albion needed somewhere local to call home while a permanent site was found. There was only one covered stand and many of the 6,000 seats were far from the pitch.

Opposition locally meant that use of the audio system was limited and there were parking restrictions within a mile of the stadium. Fans were encouraged to use public transport and possession of a matchday ticket allowed for unlimited bus travel locally.

During Albion's twelve-year tenure at the Withdean Stadium, the capacity was increased to over 8,000 by adding further temporary stands. Restrictions on the matchday sound system were also eased.

The first game at the Withdean Stadium was on 7th August 1999. On a glorious sunny day local lad Darren Freeman scored a hat-trick as Albion beat Mansfield 6-0 in front of 5,882 spectators.

Albion's stay at the Withdean Stadium may have been longer than initially anticipated and it was one of the worst venues in the Football League, but it was still home. It kept the club afloat and had many happy memories for fans who enjoyed four promotions whilst there.

FACT 72

2000
BOBBY ZAMORA

One of the most prolific strikers in Albion's history joined the club in 2000.

Bobby Zamora spent three months on loan at Albion from Bristol Rovers in the second half of the 1999/00 season. He scored six goals in six games and for most of the close season manager Micky Adams tried to secure his signing on a permanent basis.

A deal was not agreed until two days before the opening fixture but it was worth the wait. Zamora scored 28 goals as Albion won the Third Division title, then the same number in 2001-02 as they won promotion again. He even earned a call up to the England Under 21 squad.

In 2002-03, when Albion were relegated from the First Division (now the Championship), Zamora still got a respectable fourteen goals. It was no surprise that Premier League clubs were interested and in July 2003 Zamora joined Tottenham for £1.5 million. This was a great return on the £100,000 outlay of three years earlier.

After playing in the Premier League for Tottenham, West Ham, Fulham and QPR, Zamora re-joined Brighton in 2015. He scored seven league goals but struggled with a hip injury. He was by now in his mid-thirties and retired from playing after his contract was not renewed in 2016.

FACT 73
2001 THIRD DIVISION CHAMPIONS

After years of turmoil, the club had something to cheer for in 2000-01 when they finished the season as champions of the Third Division.

Albion lost three of their first four games but a 6-2 home win over Torquay on 2nd September 2000 was the first of nine games unbeaten. They retained a remarkable consistency for the rest of the season, winning nineteen of their 23 home games. It wasn't May, after the title was secured, that they again went two games without winning.

Promotion was confirmed with six games remaining. Albion won 2-0 at Plymouth then received the news that Rochdale and Hartlepool had both slipped up, meaning the celebrations could begin.

Manager Micky Adams promised to keep going and try to secure the title, paying tribute to fans who had supported the club through thick and thin during thirteen years in the basement divisions.

Adams delivered his promise on 1st May when Albion beat Chesterfield 1-0 at the Withdean Stadium to secure top spot. Adams said afterwards, "What a night! I cannot pay my players enough accolades. I've got a smashing group of players, great staff and great supporters. How could I fail."

FACT 74
2002
BACK-TO-BACK PROMOTIONS

Brighton won a second successive promotion in 2001-02. They overcame a managerial change to finish the season as champions of the Second Division.

Albion lost just two of their first twelve games. However, in October manager Micky Adams left the club to join Premier League Leicester as assistant to Dave Bassett. He was replaced by Peter Taylor, who kept the momentum going and Albion didn't lose again until January.

Bobby Zamora was again prolific, scoring 28 goals as he had done the previous season. The last of these was a superb half volley at Peterborough on 6th April that sent 4,000 Albion fans wild and left them on the brink of promotion with two games to go.

The following day, Reading could only draw with Tranmere meaning Albion couldn't finish outside the top two. A week later, they wrapped up the Second Division title with a 0-0 draw against Swindon at the Withdean Stadium.

It had been a remarkable turnaround in fortunes for the club in the last five years. However, Taylor opted not to extend his contract and left for Hull City. He was replaced by youth team manager Martin Hinshlewood for Albion's first campaign in the second tier since 1992.

FACT 75

2003
STRAIGHT BACK DOWN

Albion found it tough going after two successive promotions. They were relegated back to the Second Division after finishing 23rd in the table.

The season started promisingly, with a 3-1 win at Burnley followed by a 0-0 draw at home to Coventry. However, Albion then lost ten games in succession, the last of these being a dismal 5-0 defeat at Crystal Palace.

Steve Coppell replaced Martin Hinshlewood as manager and despite the poor form, at the turn of the year Albion's position was not a hopeless one. In February three straight wins lifted them out of the relegation zone but it was tight at the bottom, with just three points separating four sides.

On 19th April a defeat at already promoted Leicester left Albion four points from safety with three games remaining. Two days later they drew 1-1 at the Withdean Stadium with Sheffield Wednesday, a result that relegated the visitors and left Albion on the brink. However, a 4-0 win over Watford coupled with a defeat for Stoke gave Albion a glimmer of hope.

On 4th May Albion needed to win at Grimsby and hope Stoke lost at home to Reading. 2,500 fans travelled north but were left disappointed when a 2-2 draw coupled with a win for Stoke sent Albion back to the Second Division.

FACT 76
2003 SEAGULLS OLDEST PLAYER

On 4th May 2003 goalkeeper Dave Beasant played for Brighton & Hove Albion against Grimsby Town aged 44 years and 45 days. It made him the club's oldest player and it was also the last game of his professional career.

When regular keeper Michel Kuipers was injured, the vastly experienced Beasant was signed on a free transfer by Steve Coppell as Albion tried to escape relegation.

Beasant played sixteen league games in all, breaking the age record each time. He endeared himself to the fans even more when he was said to have slept in the corner of a kebab shop after a midweek victory over Crystal Palace.

The match at Grimsby was the 775th league game for a career that stretched back to 1980 when he made his debut for Wimbledon. Albion needed a victory to have any hope of avoiding relegation, but it was not to be and the game ended 2-2.

Had Coppell not signed Ben Roberts, who had been at Albion on loan from Charlton, Beasant may well have stayed at the club for 2003-04. Instead, he was with Premier League Fulham, although didn't make any further appearances.

FACT 77
2004
BACK UP
VIA THE PLAYOFFS

The Seagulls won promotion at the first attempt in 2003-04. They finished fourth in the Second Division and then triumphed in the playoffs, beating Bristol City in Cardiff.

Apart from a run of three successive defeats in which they failed to score a goal; Albion had a consistently steady season. They remained in the playoff positions throughout but finished six points off an automatic promotion spot.

In the first leg of their semi-final Albion won 1-0 at Swindon but in the return at the Withdean Stadium, trailed 2-0 in extra time. In the dying seconds, Adam Virgo scored with a diving header to force a penalty shootout, which Albion won 4-3.

Due to Wembley Stadium being rebuilt, the final was at Cardiff's Millennium Stadium. City had more of the possession but struggled to break down a tight Albion defence. It was Albion who came closest to scoring in the first half, when Leon Knight's free kick bounded off the bar.

The second half was also one of few chances. However, nine minutes from time Chris Iwelumo was brought down in the box and Knight kept his cool to convert the spot kick. Albion held on to secure promotion to the First Division, which was rebranded The Championship before the new season started.

FACT 78

2004
A GOAL AFTER TWELVE SECONDS

The fastest recorded goal by a Brighton player was scored by Maheta Molango on 7th August 2004. The Swiss striker found the net after just twelve seconds against Reading at the Madejski Stadium but never scored for Albion again.

Molango had a trial for Albion in the summer of 2004 after being released by German Second Division side Wacker Berghausen. The 22-year-old impressed with four goals in three pre-season appearances and signed a three-year deal.

Albion had a tough opening game of the 2004-05 season at Reading, one of the favourites for promotion. Straight from the kick-off Adam Virgo launched the ball forward and when the home defenders failed to clear properly, Molango took his chance and scored with a low drive.

Within two minutes Reading had equalised and the game eventually ended in a 3-2 defeat for Albion. It turned out to be as good as it got for Molango, who was dropped by Mark McGhee after just five more appearances. Between then and the end of his contract, he made one League Cup appearance and was loaned out four times.

FACT 79
2005
LAST GASP ESCAPE
FROM RELEGATION

Brighton escaped relegation by the skin of their teeth in 2004-05. In the bottom three with five games remaining, they avoided defeat in all of them to finish one point above the drop zone.

At the beginning of March Albion were in fifteenth place, ten points above the relegation zone. However, they then lost six games in succession and dropped into the bottom three.

Albion drew their next three games but remained in deep trouble. Then in the penultimate game of the season they won 1-0 at already relegated Rotherham, meaning their fate was in their own hands going into the final day.

On 8th May Albion needed a point against Ipswich Town at the Withdean Stadium to guarantee safety. Things got off to the worst possible start when the visitors, who had an outside chance of automatic promotion, went 1-0 up after four minutes. Adam Virgo equalised for Albion after ten minutes, but Albion struggled to create further chances.

In the second half Ipswich played four up front and threw everything they could at Albion, who defended courageously and held on for a draw. There were tears of joy at the end as Albion had achieved what many thought was impossible at the start of the season, staying in the Championship.

FACT 80

2005
FIRST WIN AT PALACE IN A GENERATION

Brighton endured a miserable season in 2005-06. However, there was one bright spot when they beat Crystal Palace at Selhurst Park for the first time in over twenty years.

Palace had won their last three fixtures and were clear favourites for this encounter, played on a Tuesday night in October. Since a 2-0 win on Boxing Day 1983, Albion had drawn one and lost four of their five games at Palace. Their most recent visit, in 2002, had resulted in a 5-0 hammering.

It was not a pretty game but was fiercely contested. After 25 minutes Albion midfielder Richard Carpenter had to go off injured after being caught by a stray arm. Despite this setback, Albion had the better of the game but were wasteful with chances.

Albion's winner came in the 78th minute when Paul McShane rose to head home a corner by Sébastien Carole. It was the Manchester United loanee's first goal of the season and couldn't have come at a better time.

In injury time Andy Johnson thought he'd equalised for Palace but the goal was ruled out for offside. At the end of the game the players, who had fought so hard for their win, enjoyed lengthy celebrations in front of the travelling Albion fans.

FACT 81
2006
BOTTOM OF
THE CHAMPIONSHIP

After narrowly avoiding relegation the previous season, The Seagulls finished bottom of the Championship in 2005-06. Their demotion to League One was confirmed with two games still to go.

Albion won just two of their first 23 games. However, thirteen of these were drawn so they weren't cut adrift at the bottom. Two wins in succession then lifted them out of the relegation zone and at New Year they were in 21st place.

A disastrous February saw Albion lose six games in a row. This was followed by three draws and by the end of March, Albion were nine points from safety with six games remaining. A 2-0 win at fellow strugglers Millwall gave them some hope but they then lost 2-0 at home to Southampton.

On 17th April, Albion faced Sheffield Wednesday, who were one place above them, at the Withdean Stadium. Albion were in 22nd place, seven points behind Wednesday and needed a win to have any hope of staying up. In front of 7,573 fans, Wednesday won 2-0, confirming Albion would be going down along with Millwall and Crewe.

Albion lost their remaining two games to end the season bottom of the table. A key problem over the campaign had been in attack, with leading scorer Colin Kazim-Richards finding the net just six times.

FACT 82

2006
BIGGEST VICTORY AT
WITHDEAN STADIUM

The club's best victory at the Withdean Stadium was on 11th November 2006. A young Albion side thrashed Northwich Victoria 8-0 in an FA Cup first round tie.

In September that year Mark McGhee was sacked as manager following a disappointing start to the season. He was replaced by Dean Wilkins, who stepped up from his position as youth team coach. For this tie against non-league opposition, he gave a chance to some of the youngsters who he had led to the quarter finals of the FA Youth Cup the previous season.

Albion took the lead after just eight minutes through Dean Cox and Jake Robinson's curling shot made it 2-0 ten minutes later. Early in the second half Northwich hit the post but after 55 minutes Robinson scored again to give Albion a commanding lead.

Alex Revell scored the fourth with a thirty-yard strike and Robinson completed his hat trick twelve minutes from time. Joe Gatting and Sam Rents scored the sixth and seventh before Cox tapped in from close range to complete the rout in the last minute.

Of Albion's scorers, only Revell had not come through the club's youth system. Albion then overcame Stafford Rangers before losing at West Ham in the third round.

FACT 83

2010
THE YOUNGEST PLAYER

On 8th May 2010 Jake Caskey became Brighton & Hove Albion's youngest ever player at the age of just sixteen years and thirteen days.

Caskey had been offered a scholarship deal with Albion the previous month. He was named on the bench for the final game of the season, against Yeovil Town at the Withdean Stadium.

With fifteen minutes remaining and Albion leading 1-0, the young midfielder came on for Chris Holroyd. Albion held on for victory to end the season in thirteenth place.

The following season he appeared as a substitute once, in an FA Cup tie at Stoke. He changed his surname to Forster-Caskey in 2011 out of respect to his stepfather. His full debut was against Southampton on 2nd January 2012, when he scored in a 3-0 victory.

Jake spent the first half of 2012-13 on loan at Oxford United to gain further experience. He was then a regular in the Albion side during 2013-14 and 2014-15. However, he made just four more appearances for the club and after loan spells at Milton Keynes and Rotherham, joined Charlton in January 2017. In total he made 82 appearances for Albion, scoring nine goals.

FACT 84

2011 LEAGUE ONE CHAMPIONS

Brighton enjoyed a memorable final season at the Withdean Stadium. They finished as Champions of League One, confirming promotion with five games to spare.

After picking up four points from their first three matches, Albion really got going in September. They began a twelve-game unbeaten run and went to the top of the table at the end of the month, remaining there all season.

Even a spell of five games without a win in November and December, when three other fixtures were postponed, failed to knock Albion off their perch. Opposition defenders had no answer to Albion's lethal attack pairing of Glenn Murray and Ashley Barnes, who got twenty-two and eighteen goals respectively.

During March Albion won all eight games meaning it became a case of when, not if, they would secure promotion. On 12th April they won a thrilling game against Dagenham & Redbridge 4-3 at Withdean to give them a sixteen-point cushion with five games to go. Four days later they clinched the championship with victory at Walsall.

After remaining unbeaten at home all season, Albion lost their last two fixtures. There were few complaints though as fans looked forward to a future in the Championship in a new home.

FACT 85

2011
FALMER

Fourteen years after leaving the Goldstone Ground, the club finally had a home to call their own in 2011. They moved to a purpose-built stadium in Falmer, a village north of Brighton.

The site was identified in the late 1990s and planning permission was granted by Brighton & Hove City Council in 2002. However, there were then five years of legal challenges due to concerns raised by Falmer Parish Council, Lewes District Council and South Downs Joint Committee.

Approval was finally given by the Secretary of State for Planning in 2007 and the three main opponents announced they would not take the matter to the High Court. This paved the way for construction to start the following year.

In 2010 a naming rights deal was agreed with the area's largest employer, so it became the American Express Community Stadium. The Amex, as it is usually known, was officially opened on 30th July 2011 for a friendly with Tottenham, who beat Albion 3-2.

On 6th August Albion beat Doncaster Rovers, who had been their final opponents at the Goldstone Ground, 2-1 in the first competitive game. The demand to see Albion in the new stadium was so high that by the end of 2012-13 the stadium's capacity had been expanded to 30,750.

FACT 86

2013
POYET SACKED AFTER PLAYOFF DEFEAT

In 2012-13 Brighton appeared in the playoffs for promotion to the topflight for the first time in 22 years. However, after defeat to arch rivals Crystal Palace Gus Poyet was sacked as manager.

Albion enjoyed a great start and were top of the league at the end of September, but seven games without a win saw them drop out of the playoff places. At the turn of the year they were eighth in the table.

A run of five straight wins lifted Albion into the playoff positions at the beginning of March. They were unbeaten in their last nine games and comfortably qualified for the playoffs, finishing in fourth and seven points ahead of Bolton in seventh.

Albion were away to Palace in the first leg of the semi-final. The game finished 0-0 with Albion defending resolutely in the second half to keep Palace at bay. Back at the Amex it was a tight first half but after the break the game opened up. Albion's hearts were broken as Wilfried Zaha scored twice for Palace to take them to the final.

In an interview after the game, Poyet criticised the lack of finances that were made available to him. He was suspended a few days later and dismissed from his role after an investigation.

FACT 87
2014 LATE SURGE TO PLAYOFFS

Under new manager Oscar Garcia, Albion had a late run of form in 2013-14 to claim a playoff spot. However, they were once again denied at the semi-final stage.

Garcia was appointed in June 2013, having just led Maccabi Tel Aviv to their first Israeli title in ten years. Albion lost their first two games under his charge but then went six unbeaten. Another mixed spell of results followed and at Christmas they were eighth in the table, but still within touching distance of the playoffs.

On 11th January Albion climbed into the playoff places for the first time of the season, only to pick up just one point from their next three games. Three successive defeats in March left them four points behind Reading with eight games remaining.

Albion remained unbeaten for the rest of the season but left it extremely late to secure their playoff place. On the last day of the season Leonardo Ulloa scored an injury time winner at Nottingham Forest allowing them to go above Reading, who could only draw their game.

Albion's efforts ended up counting for nothing. After losing 2-1 at home to Derby in the first leg of the playoff semi-final, they went down 4-1 at Pride Park to lose 6-2 on aggregate.

FACT 88
2015
HUGHTON SAVES ALBION FROM RELEGATION

After two playoff appearances, the club had a dismal season in 2014-15. They looked to be heading for relegation but a managerial change saw Sami Hyypia replaced by Chris Hughton, who led them to safety.

When Oscar Garcia resigned following a second successive playoffs defeat, he was replaced by former Liverpool defender Hyypia. He had led Bayer Leverkusen to two top four finishes in the Bundesliga and there was plenty of cause for optimism.

Albion won just three out of their first 23 matches. Hyypia was sacked on 22nd December with Albion in the relegation zone. He was quickly replaced by Hughton, who oversaw a steady climb up the table, with just two defeats in a ten-game spell during February and March.

Despite failing to win any of their last seven matches, Albion comfortably avoided the drop by finishing six points ahead of Millwall. Their road to safety had also been helped by the presence in the Championship of a Blackpool side who had the joint worst points total of a 24 team second tier.

Hughton knew there was further room for improvement though. After a 2-0 defeat to Watford in the last home game, he promised reinforcements for the following season so Albion could be back competing at the top end of the table.

FACT 89
2015 RECORD UNBEATEN RUN

In 2015 a club record run of 22 league games without defeat was achieved.

The run started when Albion drew 0-0 at Middlesbrough in the last game of 2014-15. They then began 2015-16 with a 1-0 home win over Nottingham Forest and 2-1 win at Fulham.

After a 1-1 draw at Huddersfield, Albion won four games in a row, all of them by the odd goal. They then drew three in succession before returning to winning ways with late winners at Leeds and against Bristol City at the Amex.

There were then another three drawn games on the bounce before a 2-1 home win over MK Dons. After a 1-1 draw at Burnley the next two games against Birmingham and Charlton were home and Albion came from behind to win them both.

Albion then conceded late equalisers at Derby and QPR. The unbeaten run of 22 games had consisted of eleven wins and eleven draws, with all of the wins being by just one goal.

The run finally came to an end on 19th December when top of the table Middlesbrough won 3-0 at the Amex. Chris Hughton was realistic afterwards, saying "It is very difficult to be too harsh on the players, the reaction from our supporters at the end was excellent."

FACT 90

2016 PROMOTION AGONY

After a 21-game unbeaten start, Brighton failed to gain promotion to the Premier League in 2015-16. They missed out on going up automatically on the last day of the season, then suffered defeat in the playoffs for the third time in four years.

Albion were top of the Championship in mid-December. However, four defeats in five games over Christmas and New Year saw them drop to sixth. They recovered to win four in succession and lost only once more all season.

On the last day of the campaign, Albion travelled to second placed Middlesbrough, who they trailed on goal difference. A win would take Albion up, but the game ended in a 1-1 draw meaning they were in the playoffs again.

Albion lost the first leg of their semi-final 2-0 at Sheffield Wednesday. In the return at the Amex, Albion started well with Anthony Knockaert hitting the post from a free kick early in the game before crossing for Lewis Dunk to halve the deficit. However, they conceded a freak equaliser before half time when a cross sailed into the net.

In the second half Albion rarely looked like turning the tie around. It ended 1-1 and Albion had missed out to a team that they had finished fifteen points ahead of in the table.

FACT 91
2017 PROMOTION TO THE PREMIER LEAGUE

The disappointment of the previous season was well and truly put behind the club as they won automatic promotion to the Premier League in 2016-17.

Albion were unbeaten in their first four games but then lost two in a row. However, they then embarked on a run of eighteen games without defeat and were never out of the top two from mid-October.

A key element to Albion's success was their consistency at home, where they won seventeen out of twenty-three games. They also had a strong defence, which conceded just forty goals, the joint fewest in the Championship.

On the afternoon of 17th April, Albion faced relegation threatened Wigan at the Amex. Glenn Murray scored from the edge of the area to put them ahead and Solly March doubled the lead early in the second half. Wigan scored late in the game but Albion held on for victory.

Afterwards supporters celebrated on the pitch even though a Premier League place was still not mathematically certain. Huddersfield were twelve points behind with four games left but had a vastly inferior goal difference. In the evening kick-off Huddersfield could only draw with Derby, confirming Albion's promotion.

In the remaining three games Albion picked up just one point but nobody was complaining as the club looked forward to a first topflight season since 1982-83.

FACT 92
2018
FIRST VAR IN
ENGLISH FOOTBALL

On 8th January 2018 the FA Cup game with Crystal Palace was the first time that Video Assistant Referee (VAR) was used in a competitive game in England.

The third-round tie was played on a Monday night and the Amex was less than half full. An unstoppable shot from Dale Stephens had given Albion a first half lead but midway through the second period Bakary Sako equalised for Palace.

With three minutes remaining Glenn Murray scored from close range after a free kick had been floated into the box. After appeals from Palace players that there had been a handball and consultation with the VAR official, referee Andre Marriner went to check the pitch side monitor. It took about fifteen seconds for Marriner to confirm that the goal stood and that the ball had in fact gone into the net off Murray's knee.

The game finished 2-1 for Albion and manager Chris Hughton was happy with how VAR was applied, saying "It's reasonably clear that it didn't hit his hand and there was no decision to be made."

FACT 93
2018
FIRST BLACK MANAGER OF MONTH

Chris Hughton was the first black Premier League Manager of the Month when he won the award for February 2018.

In their first season back in the topflight after 34 years, Albion lost their first two games. They then lost two of their next ten and were in twelfth place at Christmas.

During February Albion were unbeaten, having impressive home wins against West Ham and Swansea. They also beat Coventry to reach the quarter finals of the FA Cup. On 4th March, they enjoyed a 2-1 win over Arsenal at the Amex, their first win over one of the 'Big Six." Hughton was the first black manager to win the award and praised his players, who he said had improved as the season went on but knew there was more work to do.

In 2018-19, Albion won just two games after the turn of the year, falling from a mid-table position to finish seventeenth, just two points above the relegation zone.

The day after the season ended, chairman Tony Bloom made the difficult decision to sack Hughton. Bloom told the media that he had done an excellent job and will always be one of Albion's finest and most respected managers but had to do what was best after a disappointing second half of the season.

FACT 94

2018
TWO FIRST HALF GOALS FROM SUBSTITUTES

History was made when Brighton beat Crystal Palace 3-1 in an eventful A23 derby on 4th December 2018. For the first time in the Premier League's history, two substitutes scored in the first half.

Albion took a 24th minute lead when Glenn Murray converted a penalty kick awarded for a foul on James McArthur. However, four minutes later he was forced off after suffering a shoulder injury in a challenge by James Tomkins. In the furore surrounding that incident, Albion's Shane Duffy was sent off for an attempted head butt.

To compensate for going down to ten men, defensive midfielder Leon Balogon came on for flare player Pascal Gross. He scored with his first touch to give Albion a 2-0 lead. In stoppage time of the first half Florin Andone — who had replaced Murray — scored the third.

There was no further scoring by Albion in the second half and Palace converted a late penalty for the game to end 3-1. It was a memorable win for Albion's fans, while the goals from Balogon and Andone as first half substitutes were a first in the Premier League.

FACT 95

2019
GLENN MURRAY'S
100TH LEAGUE GOAL

On 9th March 2019 Glenn Murray scored in Albion's 2-1 win at Crystal Palace. It his 100th league goal for Albion, making him the first player to reach that total since Tommy Cook in the 1920s.

Murray spent four seasons with Albion between 2007 and 2011, all of them in League One. During that spell he scored 54 league goals before moving to Palace, who were then in the Championship. He left there in 2015 and signed for Bournemouth, before returning to Albion a year later, initially on loan.

In January 2017 Murray's loan was made permanent and he finished the season with 23 goals as Albion were promoted to the Premier League. He then scored twelve goals in 2017-18 and the following season he featured in every league game, netting thirteen times.

Murray's 100th league goal for Albion was in the nineteenth minute and opened the scoring in a 2-1 win over Palace at Selhurst Park. For the first time in over ninety years, an Albion player had reached a league century and unlike Cook, not all of Murray's goals had been in the lower divisions.

During 2019-20 Murray struggled for form and managed just one league goal. At the start of 2020-21, by which time he was near his 37th birthday, he was loaned to Watford and in the January transfer window signed for Nottingham Forest.

FACT 96
2019 FA CUP SEMI FINALISTS

2018-19 saw the best run in the FA Cup since being beaten finalists in 1983 when the club reached the semi-final, where they were beaten 1-0 by Manchester City.

In the 3rd round Albion won 3-1 at Bournemouth, before needing a replay to beat West Bromwich Albion in the 4th round. After a 0-0 draw at the Amex, Albion won 3-1 in the replay at The Hawthorns. They then beat Derby County 2-1 at home in the 5th round.

Albion were drawn away to Millwall in the 6th round. They looked to be heading out of the competition when they trailed 2-0 with less than five minutes remaining. However, Jürgen Locadia scored with two minutes to go then in the fifth minute of injury time Solly March equalised with a free kick. Thirty minutes of extra time couldn't decide the tie and Albion triumphed 5-4 on penalties.

In the semi-final Albion faced Premier League leaders Manchester City at Wembley on 6th April. They were a goal down after just four minutes and although City were way below their best, Albion couldn't capitalise on this. There were few chances for either side and the game ended 1-0 for City, who went on to beat Watford in the final.

FACT 97
2019 RECORD WOMEN'S SUPER LEAGUE CROWD

On 28th April 2019 a record-breaking Women's Super League crowd of 5,265 watched a match against Arsenal at the Amex.

Although Albion struggled in their first season at the top level, relegation was never likely due to Yeovil having had a huge points deduction.

Home games were usually played at Crawley Town, but the last one of the season was switched to the Amex Stadium. With Arsenal having a chance of securing the title, a record crowd was anticipated. The attendance of 5,265 broke the previous record by more than 200.

Arsenal took a sixth minute lead and after that the result was never in doubt. They dominated the game and cruised to a 4-0 victory, their seventeenth of the season from nineteen games played.

Albion's manager Hope Powell said afterwards, "We did our best to try and spoil their party but, for us, it was a massive learning curve against a top-quality side and we have to find the positives from it. For a lot of these players, it's their first time being in a professional environment. I think we've done fantastically well considering where we've come from."

The record crowd only lasted until later in the year, when a round of matches on an international weekend were played at the club's main stadiums.

FACT 98

2020
SURVIVAL BEHIND
CLOSED DOORS

Brighton finished fifteenth in 2019-20, securing a fourth successive season in the Premier League. In a season that was disrupted by the Covid-19 pandemic, they secured survival in their final home game of the season, which like four others was played behind closed doors.

Albion were fifteenth, two points above the drop zone when the season was suspended in March with nine games remaining. When it resumed behind closed doors in June, Albion beat Arsenal 2-1 at the Amex in their first game back.

A 1-0 win at doomed Norwich on 4th July meant Albion opened up a nine-point gap between themselves and the bottom three with five games left. However, they were well beaten at home by Liverpool and Manchester City, meaning there was still work to do.

Albion could have secured safety with a win at Southampton on 16th July but had to settle for a 1-1 draw after Neal Maupay had put them ahead. Four days later, Albion drew 0-0 at home to Newcastle to secure their topflight status.

In the last game of the season, Albion won 2-1 at Burnley, meaning they finished fifteenth and seven points clear of Bournemouth who went down along with Watford and Norwich.

FACT 99
2020
HITTING THE
WOODWORK RECORD

A late 3-2 defeat by Manchester United on 26th September 2020 was even more heart-breaking as it set an unwanted record. Albion hit the woodwork five times, more than anyone else since Opta began recording statistics in 2004.

In an eventful first half, Leandro Trossard hit the post in the ninth and 21st minute with shots from outside the box. After half an hour, Adam Webster's looping header beat keeper David de Gea but hit the bar.

Albion took the lead through Neal Maupay five minutes before half time, but an own goal by Lewis Dunk meant the sides were level at the break.

Ten minutes into the second half Marcus Rashford put United ahead then on the hour mark Solly March's effort hit the post. Albion hit the woodwork for the fifth time in the 76th minute when Trossard's effort struck the bar.

Four minutes into injury time March headed an equaliser. The game looked to have finished 2-2, but in an astonishing development after the final whistle, a penalty was awarded to United for a handball by Maupay following a VAR review. This was converted by Bruno Fernandes leaving Albion devastated.

Not only had they hit the woodwork five times, but they had also been denied a penalty themselves by VAR after the referee had pointed to the spot.

FACT 100
2021 CHAMPION VICTORIES

Brighton finished 16th in 2020-21 to secure a fifth straight season in the Premier League. Memorable moments in Covid hit season included a first victory over reigning champions Liverpool at Anfield for 39 years, and a win over new champions Manchester City in the last home game of the season.

On 3rd February Steven Alzate's goal gave Albion a 1-0 victory over 2020's runaway champions Liverpool at an empty Anfield, where they had not won since 1982. It was the second home defeat in a week for Liverpool, having previously gone nearly four years without losing in the league at Anfield.

The victory at Anfield was Albion's fourth of the season, all of them away from home at the time. They had really struggled playing at the Amex Stadium behind closed doors and didn't win there until 20th March, when Newcastle were beaten 3-0. This helped put some daylight between Albion and the bottom three and they were safe from relegation with three games remaining.

On 18th May Albion played newly crowned champions Manchester City at the Amex. Easing of Covid restrictions meant that a crowd of 8,000 was allowed inside. They were 2-0 down early in the second half but hit back to win 3-2. The winner was scored by Dan Burn, his first goal for three years, ending a difficult season on a high note.

The 100 Facts Series

Arsenal, *Steve Horton*	978-1-908724-09-0
Aston Villa, *Steve Horton*	978-1-908724-98-4
Brighton, *Steve Horton*	978-1-912782-78-9
Celtic, *Steve Horton*	978-1-908724-10-6
Chelsea, *Kristian Downer*	978-1-908724-11-3
Everton, *Bob Sharp*	978-1-908724-12-0
Hearts, *Steve Horton*	978-1-912782-48-2
Leeds, *Steve Horton*	978-1-908724-94-6
Leicester City, *Steve Horton*	978-1-912782-47-5
Liverpool, *Steve Horton*	978-1-908724-13-7
Manchester City, *Steve Horton*	978-1-908724-14-4
Manchester United, *Iain McCartney*	978-1-908724-15-1
Newcastle United, *Steve Horton*	978-1-908724-16-8
Norwich City, *Steve Horton*	978-1-908724-99-1
Nottingham Forest, *Steve Horton*	978-1-912782-46-8
Rangers, *David Clayton*	978-1-908724-17-5
Sheffield United, *Steve Horton*	978-1-912782-45-1
Southampton, *Steve Horton*	978-1-912782-79-6
Sunderland, *Steve Horton*	978-1-912782-80-2
Tottenham Hotspur, *Steve Horton*	978-1-908724-18-2
West Ham, *Steve Horton*	978-1-908724-80-9

Player Autographs

Player Autographs

Player Autographs

Player Autographs